CW00926602

'Taking on the responsibility of leading and executing a c
cripple even the most talented of designers, so it's excitii
creative side of the industry tackling the business challer
get forgotten in education and that rely all too heavily on
Johnson's book offers sharp insights into improving knowleuge anu skills, and
building effective practices to enable success. It's a book not only for the benefit of
the reader, but the teams they manage and the creative sparks within.'
STEPHEN HOLMES, Editor DEVELOP3D Magazine

'Design Lead Succeed is a no-nonsense guide for designers and creatives who are
tackling the difficult leap from talented designer to team leader. Having witnessed
Chris's journey first-hand there is no one more qualified to support you along that
journey. His hard-earned wisdom and success has created a companion book you'll
revisit time after time.'
JOSEPH SANTRY, Senior Director Futures Innovation, lululemon

'I have years of experience in the field of design, both in industry and academia, but I
still found Chris's book thought provoking and challenging for my practice. I wish I
had been able to read it years ago as it would have supported me throughout my
progression in the workplace.'
SIMON PATTISON, Course Lead in Product Design, York St John University

'The 48 rules that Chris presents would take any design leader years of dedicated
effort to amass, each time having to work through a personal, yet avoidable, 'teaching
moment' to unlock every invaluable insight themselves. Having this book at your
disposal is akin to having Chris, an experienced Red Dot award winner and
accomplished design leader on your own team, guiding you to creative and leadership
success, pointing out the pitfalls, and providing the tools to overcome them.'
ROSS WEIR, Innovation Director, Progressive Sports Technologies Ltd.

'Chris's approach offers creative, strategic, and practical solutions applicable across
various product areas. Each of the 48 rules is presented in a concise, easily digestible
format, suitable for designers at any career stage.'
JAMES HOLT, Product Design Director, Antler

**48 RULES FOR BRIDGING
THE GAP FROM DESIGNER
TO DESIGN LEADER**

DESIGN
LEAD
SUCCEED

Laura,
I hope you enjoy this book.
Best wishes,
Chris Johnson.
06.02.2024

CHRIS
JOHNSON

Chris Johnson
Design Ltd

To Luke, Bethany, Cathy, and my parents

Find me here
www.chrisjohnson.design

First paperback edition November 2023

ISBN 978-1-7395492-0-6 (hardback)
ISBN 978-1-7395492-1-3 (paperback)
ISBN 978-1-7395492-2-0 (ebook)

www.chrisjohnson.design

CONTENTS

48 RULES

FOR BRIDGING THE GAP FROM DESIGNER TO DESIGN LEADER

SECTION

RULES

PAGE

③

HOW TO CURATE AND LEAD YOUR A TEAM

SECTION   RULES   PAGE

4   **18-33**   **114**

HOW TO BE A GREAT DESIGN LEADER

SECTION **5**   RULES **34-48**   PAGE **182**

HOW TO ELEVATE THE DESIGN CREATION PROCESS

'Whether you're taking your first steps into management, a seasoned leader, or building a team from the ground up, this book is your blueprint for fostering creativity within organisations'

CHRIS JOHNSON

INTRODUCTION

still remember the feeling of foreboding I experienced before taking on responsibility for managing a group of designers for the first time. I was a senior designer with over 10 years of experience, and I was well-practised in the process of leading designers through a project. But leading as a line manager, with responsibility for the vision and continued success of an organisation's product category design, was another level. I had always envisaged that this situation would arise one day on my career path, so I had tried to prepare in advance. I frequently read up on design management topics, and I even acquired an MBA after a few tough years of part-time study. I had a bunch of theories and a bag of tricks in my back pocket, all of which I thought would help me navigate my way through this new challenge of leading a creative team. Although these helped me in many ways, study couldn't fully prepare me for the experience of being a design manager. My evolution was instead driven by real-world experience which provided me with some hard-earned management street smarts. This was the start of my journey of discovering how to lead people in the pursuit of maximum creativity.

And this is what this book is all about. It aims to crystallise the insights I have accrued throughout my years as a design leader into 48 'rules'. They capture the essence of my process, refined over many years. It's about what works and what doesn't. It's about the foundations you need to thrive and how to progress and evolve. It's about the science and the art of design and management. It's about what happens on the ground as a design manager – the reality of the job.

All of these rules are focused around hints and tips rather than a deep dive into the theory. I want to give you a quick reference guide: pointers for when you need to take immediate action on the go. Every rule in this book is also tried and tested – I've successfully implemented all of them at one time or another in my career.

They're designed to help you establish a high-performing team capable of creating compelling concepts which develop into amazing products and commercial success. Think of them as the 20% of activity which delivers 80% of the results, as embodied by the Pareto principle.

The book is separated into five themed sections that chart the process of becoming an outstanding design leader: Section 1: *How to Know Yourself, Your Organisation and Your Industry;* Section 2: *How to Develop a Powerful Mission and Ethos;* Section 3: *How to Curate and Lead Your A Team;* Section 4: *How to Become a Great Design Leader;* and Section 5: *How to Elevate the Design Creation Process.* The intention is that each part builds on the last to help form solid foundations for your leadership. It's important to begin with Section 1 because knowing yourself and understanding the bigger picture allows you to be less reactive and more proactive. You'll be able to understand the challenges and constraints as well as the opportunities and how to leverage your assets as you form your plans. Section 2 and Section 3 focus on setting up your design team in the best way possible to maximise creativity and productivity. Finally, Section 4 and Section 5 explore approaches to leading the creative process and carrying out creative activities in order to build the best possible products.

But you don't have to be a designer or even from the creative industries to benefit from the contents of this book. You could be in your first management role, an experienced manager and organisational leader, or even starting to build a business or team from scratch. All those who manage people will benefit from the rules shared here. This book is about setting up teams within organisations and allowing creativity to thrive, written from the practitioner's perspective. Moreover, even within the world of design, this book covers a breadth of design team scenarios. I feel fortunate to have experience in both design consultancies and within the in-house design teams of various global brands. I've designed products as large as trains and aircraft interiors and as small as swimming tracking devices and ear plugs. I've worked in small business start-ups, SMEs and large global organisations. And the rules within this book apply to all of those design contexts.

Ignore those people who declare that great leaders are born that way and have intrinsic qualities. Whether you are currently a designer considering a leadership career or you've been thrust into the role, I believe you can become a great design leader. You must only decide to commit to embracing the endless challenge of uncertainty, seek to continually learn and improve your knowledge and skills, and most importantly, desire to not only serve your own interests and those of your organisation but to actively serve the people within your care; and, when I say care, I mean truly care for their best interests and futures. Your dedication to care and empathy will be recognised by others as authenticity, which will help you to build trust, commitment and loyalty. If you look after the people in your team, you'll build a reputation for being a leader who people want to join, and it'll be easier to attract talented individuals.

I sincerely hope that you enjoy reading the following chapters and that it helps to elevate your design leadership performance.

Good luck and all the very best on your creative journey,

Chris

ABOUT THE
AUTHOR

'As the design leader, you carry the crucial role of forging an operational system that not only steers and oversees the creative journey from start to finish but also ensures its consistent execution and continuous improvement.'

CHRIS JOHNSON

CHRIS JOHNSON

is an award-winning designer and innovation leader with over 25 years of international experience working for global brands. Born and raised in Durham, England, he completed his Bachelor of Arts in Transport Design at Coventry University in 1998. He moved to London soon after and became a design consultant for his first five years in the industry. He has worked as an in-house designer for the past 20 years, working his way up the ranks from senior designer to design manager, design lead, head of design, and design director. He is the co-inventor of various sports technology patents relating to garments, equipment and digital devices, and he has created product innovations that have helped athletes attain Olympic titles and world records. His work has been awarded Red Dot design awards and has been exhibited in collections such as the Design Museum in London. Chris has an MBA with distinction from Durham University Business School, and he is a fellow of the Royal Society for Arts, Manufactures and Commerce (RSA).

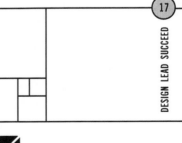

Find me here
www.chrisjohnson.design

SECTION

HOW TO KNOW YOURSELF, YOUR ORGANISATION AND YOUR INDUSTRY

How can you ever expect to achieve success if you have limited knowledge of your organisation, the market it operates in and your own design leadership qualities? Inner reflection and research on what's around you and what's at your disposal will help you to better understand the improvements that are necessary to become world-class and then, ultimately, world-best.

By acquiring a clearer understanding of your present and future challenges and opportunities, you will be empowered to shift gears and operate with foresight and conviction, at a higher level of leadership!

The following rules in this section of the book will help you to make that leap and fulfil your promise.

DESIGN LEAD SUCCEED

1 DISCOVER WHO YOU ARE

'The more you know yourself, the more clarity there is.'

JIDDU KRISHNAMURTI

What Is the Rule?

Knowing who you are – your beliefs, behaviours and personality traits – and how you best function provides a foundation from which to better navigate and orchestrate the ever-changing situations around you. Decision-making is a critical task that leaders must competently carry out each day, and understanding yourself well helps you to intuitively make better decisions, which results in greater success.

The Problem

Imagine the difference between a racing driver trying to set a lap record in an untested car on an unfamiliar track compared to one who is familiar with both. If the second driver already has experience of the track's bends and crunch points and the handling capabilities of the car, then this scenario should result in a faster lap! They will know how to maximise its potential. Similarly, possessing a greater awareness of yourself and your natural traits and tendencies helps you to navigate life more efficiently and successfully. You will be able to build better relationships with your team and the wider organisation. For example, building your team and its organisational structure should be a simpler task if you're already clear on your own strengths and weaknesses as you can shape the team in a complementary manner. But truly knowing yourself is difficult and could even be considered an endless process, as you continually grow and develop as a person and as a leader. If you are to excel, though, however painful it is, you must try to continually uncover your blind spots to gain a clearer understanding of who you are.

The Solution

So, how do we assess who we are? As a starting point, we can consider ourselves as being made up of our mind (psychological abilities) and body (physiological abilities). When combined, the mind and body produce our technical skills (capabilities).

To successfully lead the creative process, it is important for you to understand your own personality – including your beliefs and behaviours – as well as your preferred ways of working as a leader. More specifically, you should have a clear understanding of your leadership style, your design philosophy and your preferred creative working practices (the technical skills areas highlighted in Figure 1.1). Let's dive into these in more detail and how to best explore them.

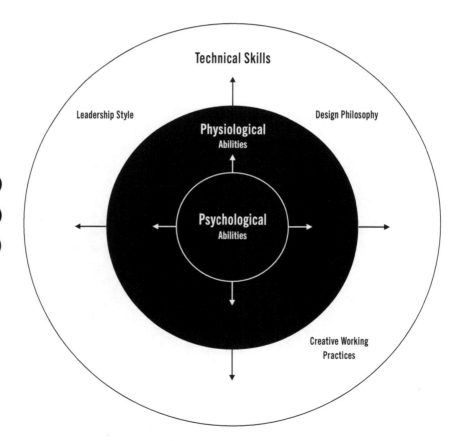

Figure 1.1 The components of a design leader

Personality

- Understand your personality type and traits so that you can effectively judge how to best interact with others. You might want to use the Myers-Briggs Type Indicator (MBTI) questionnaire or something similar.
- What motivates and drives you? This knowledge can be a great way to check that your career path has not meandered off track.
- Do you have a mentor or a close associate with whom you can explore the unknown aspects of your approach?
- Do you know when you're most productive with creative and administrative tasks? For example, is it when you're working in the early morning or in the afternoon? This knowledge allows you to effectively organise your working schedule.

Leadership style

- What's your management style? For example, is your innate approach to be more autocratic or democratic?
- How do you provide effective feedback in creative reviews to your team?
- How do you inspire and motivate your team?
- What makes you different from other leaders? Use your personal story and career journey as a way of differentiating yourself and becoming memorable. This is important because it helps you to stand out in the minds of others, such as your team, clients and the owner of the business.

Design philosophy

- This is your point of view and your unique style when it comes to design.
- Write down and define your approach to the creative process. What are your design values and principles?
- Being clear on your values – both personal and in relation to design – can be invaluable. Regardless of what your personal list is, it's advantageous to include 'integrity'. Without integrity, we might not be intentionally acting in the best interests of our team, society and the environment.

Creative working practices

- How do you prefer to work to produce the best results? For example, do you prefer to begin a design project by methodically planning each stage, or do you prefer to dive straight in with a more organic and less regimented approach? Do you prefer to ideate by sketching your ideas on paper, working directly in CAD or creating a model prototype with your hands?
- Where do your skill strengths lie? Continue to build on these.

- Where do your skill weaknesses lie? You can seek to eliminate these weaknesses, but in the meantime, be acutely aware of when they may impact your work and adjust accordingly.
- What's in your bag of tricks? For example, which tried and tested methods do you use for design research, design concept filtering and evaluation, or facilitating ideation sessions with your team of designers or design managers?

Drawing It All Together

By exploring your foundations – your beliefs, behaviours and personality traits – you can become clearer about who you really are. This journey will help you to discover your leadership style, design philosophy and preferred creative working practices, all of which have a big impact on your approach as a design leader. Equipped with this self-knowledge, you'll operate in a more effective and consistent manner, which will instil trust and confidence in those around you.

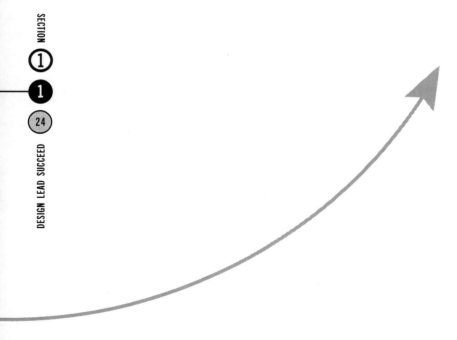

2 FIND THE SECRET SAUCE

'If you don't have a competitive advantage, don't compete.'

JACK WELCH

What Is the Rule?

You need to understand the unique value of your organisation and product, as well as their limitations, in order to thrive. It will become clear whether you possess a competitive advantage after carrying out your own analysis of the organisation's internal workings. Identifying your brand's particular personality and product proposition, as well as your team's specific design capabilities, allows you to protect, build and exploit that competitive advantage. However, you can only make inroads here if you and your team are given the influence and support to shape the future of the company.

The Problem

Without a clear understanding of the value of your organisation, the brand and the product, you will not be in a position from which to move forward and become more successful. Whether you are new to the organisation or already in the design leadership role, it's important to spend time on this analysis. Your 'secret sauce' could be in any area, from the culture of the organisation to the manufacturing process. Identifying your unique approach or capability will help to differentiate your product in the marketplace and set it apart from (and ideally above) your competitors.

However, you need a certain level of power in order to bring about improvements. As the design leader, you need to be aware of how the organisation operates and takes the product to market but also, critically, how your design team contributes to this process. You need to understand the reach of design within the organisation. What do you control, what can you influence and what is outside of your control? The answers to these questions will tell you how successful your organisation could become. A recent analysis of over 300 publicly listed companies by the management consultancy McKinsey & Company found a strong correlation between 'design-led' companies and superior business performance. Their research identified that these 'design-led' companies delivered 32% higher revenue growth and 56% higher total returns to shareholder growth.

In industries where the user is the shopper, for example when someone buys clothes from a high street store that they are going to wear themselves or gift to someone else, aesthetics are much more important because they help to influence our emotions, which ultimately drive the purchasing decision. The leading consumer brands and products are succeeding because they are design-led businesses. These brands recognise the importance of good design, and, therefore, it touches every part of the consumer experience. To do this successfully, they respect the value of design internally within their organisations, and they provide these teams with the level of control and influence they need. An indicator of a design-led business might be a design leader at the executive level or C-suite of a business. This individual may be called the 'chief design officer', 'vice president of design' or 'creative director'. Ideally, this individual will be you! It will give you the authority to direct every visual aspect of the brand and every consumer touchpoint, including visual identity, product, packaging, marketing communications, retail interior design and online visual presence. In this way, you can ensure a consistent visual identity: the look and feel of the brand. Without a design leader taking this role in the upper echelons of the organisation, a brand may underperform because of disjointed-looking product ranges, branding and marketing campaigns etc. This is a true indicator of the power and influence of design. The companies' priorities lie elsewhere if this isn't the case.

The Solution

To gain a clearer understanding of how your organisation and design team performs internally, you can use the SWOT analysis tool (Figure 2.1) and list the areas which you believe to be 'strengths' and 'weaknesses'.

As suggested, it is advantageous to consider the organisation and its brand, or brands, as a whole, but then also your design team, to ensure you build a full picture of the business. The areas to analyse could be grouped into the following categories:

1. The business set-up and its operating model.
2. The shoppers, consumers and customers the business serves.
3. The product propositions.

Strengths Business Operating Model Shopper, Consumer, Customer Product Propositions Design Creation Go to Market	**Weaknesses** Business Operating Model Shopper, Consumer, Customer Product Propositions Design Creation Go to Market
Opportunities	Threats

Figure 2.1 SWOT analysis of the internal workings of your business

4. How the product propositions are designed and manufactured.
5. How the product propositions are taken to market.

In order to analyse how your business works and where its strengths and weaknesses lie, consider these questions within the five categories just outlined.

The business set-up and its operating model
• Who owns and runs the business, and who does it serve?
• Why does it exist, and what is its purpose or mission statement? When did it commence trading? Does your brand have heritage and a story to tell which instils confidence and authenticity and which can be leveraged?
• What's most important to the owners of the organisation? Is it that the product is reliable, that the business keeps generating an adequate level of profit or that the product and company transform and revolutionise the industry for the benefit of the consumer?
• What services and products does it sell? What is its corporate,

business, marketing and product strategy? What is its operating model (direct-to-consumer, business-to-business or both?)

● What is the culture of the business? Is it driven by the sales and marketing team or the product team? Or could it even be design-led?

● How does it view and utilise 'design'? Is design central to the strategy? Understand how much value is placed on the implementation of design in the operating model.

● What is the level of appetite for risk in terms of product design and innovation? The purpose and mission statement of the organisation should provide some sort of clue as to how ambitious and risk-orientated they are.

● Are you the market leader?

● What is the ambition and strategy of the business? Is it a start-up in a new market with ambitious growth plans, or is it a mature company in a mature market, planning for steady growth?

The shoppers, consumers and customers the business serves

● Who are the shoppers, consumers and customers and how well do you serve them? Because we're considering direct-to-consumer and business-to-business operations, it helps to use the terms 'shopper', 'consumer' and 'customer' for clarity. For example, if someone is looking to buy a watch, they are a 'shopper'. If they buy the watch and then use it themselves, they become the end user or 'consumer'. If they gift the watch to someone else, that person will become the 'consumer' instead. The term 'customer' is often all-encompassing and used to describe both the shopper and the end user, or consumer, of a product. But, for clarity, here we'll consider the 'customer' as another business. For example, a retailer of watches would be the 'customer' if they purchase watches from a watch manufacturer to sell onto end users or consumers.

The product propositions

● Does the current product fulfil the needs and wants of the consumer, or is it lacking?

● If you have competitors, what is it that differentiates your designs and business?

● What is the perceived quality of the design of your products to the consumer?

● What product features have more prominence and are considered superior to your competitors' products by your consumers? For example, GORE-TEX is a layered fabric technology which provides insulation while also allowing water repellency and thermoregulation. Not all companies have licensee agreements with GORE-TEX to use their fabric technology in their products, but those that do benefit because GORE-TEX has proven benefits which are recognised by consumers.

How the product propositions are designed and manufactured

• Is there a creative director with overall autonomy and control over all aesthetic consumer touchpoints?

• Is there an intentional and consistent design language applied across all products?

• If you sell products, then how do you manufacture them? Is it a vertical business with its own manufacturing capabilities, or does it use external manufacturers?

• What intellectual property does it own, and does it possess a patent portfolio?

• What are the resources at your disposal in terms of time, cost, quality and proprietary technologies?

• What's special about your product and how it's designed? How strong is it? Is there a strength in a particular part of the design process?

• Is there a unique aspect to the design process or manufacturing process which competitors can't replicate?

• How strong is the design team? Where do the strengths of the design team lie? Is there potential that still hasn't been tapped into? For example, does the operating business model hold them back, or is there an unwillingness to invest in and value the contribution of design?

• Who gets final sign-off of the product design before it goes to market?

• Is overall design consistency, brand alignment and quality of product considered as highly as target cost?

How the product propositions are taken to market

• Where does the business trade? Is it local or global? What are its key markets? For example, which regions of the world generally deliver the most profit or experience the highest growth, or which have the greatest potential for growth or form part of the business strategy for that particular planning period?

• Where does the business sell to consumers? For example, what are its mix of retail channels, both in-store and online?

Once you have your list of strengths and weaknesses, you can then begin to filter and utilise that information by exploring how you could 'build' on your areas of strength and 'eliminate' some of the weaknesses. After this exercise, you should have a good general overview of what is going on. Then it is important to prioritise the areas for immediate action. Consider which could have the greatest impact on improving the product proposition.

It's important to understand that there will be limits to what improvements you can make. The greater the remit and control of the design function within the business, the greater the changes you will be able to enact. But there will be aspects which you can only hope to influence and even those which are totally out of your control. Take a look at Figure 2.2, which helps you analyse and categorise each strength and weakness by your influence over it.

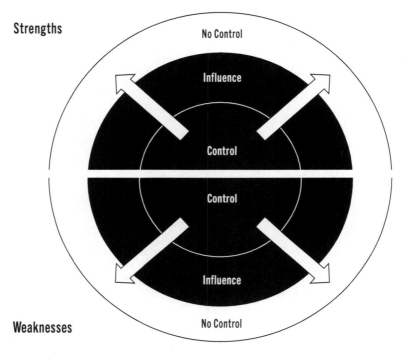

Figure 2.2 Defining your level of control over the strengths and weaknesses

Test the list of strengths and weaknesses with colleagues to understand if you have missed any major aspects. It serves as a tool that can be continually updated.

If you are new to the business, your initial evaluation may need to be refined and tested once you have had sufficient time to get to know your role and the organisation. However, there is great benefit in having a fresh perspective, so hold on to those initial insights. Once you are inside the business, it's much harder to step outside of your familiar surroundings and look at things objectively.

Drawing It All Together

Getting to know the competitive advantages and limitations of your organisation helps you to chart a course of improvement. It's critical to understand how you rank against your competitors in order to stand out in the marketplace. Focus on the aspects within your control and those you can influence.

What is your 'secret sauce'? What differentiates you and makes you unique? You want to improve in all areas, but it's also important to understand where the brand, product proposition and the design team shine in particular. What do your competitors not have, and what would they find hard to copy? When you find this, capitalise on it.

3 UNDERSTAND WHAT WORKED BEFORE

'The longer you can look back, the farther you can look forward.'
WINSTON CHURCHILL

What Is the Rule?

Unless you are working in a start-up, you will be taking on a design leadership role that's been occupied before. Reinventing the wheel is not always necessary, especially when your predecessors may have already built effective systems and accomplished success. So, learn what went before, as well as what worked and what didn't, to avoid wasting time creating new processes and repeating unnecessary mistakes.

The Problem

Time is a scarce resource, and expectations of you are high when beginning a new role as a design leader in a well-established organisation. You are the newcomer. You are a stranger to the team, a stranger to their existing social norms and behaviours, and critically, you are a stranger to how these people were previously led. Yes, you will have a new plan that you want to implement – and perhaps that your new bosses hired you for – but you should prepare to meet possible resistance somewhere down the line. And you may repeat mistakes made by previous leaders if you don't fully appreciate and understand the history of your role.

When the opportunity arose to lead my former organisation's design function, I was in an advantageous position to understand 'what went before' and what delivered success. Over the previous decade, I had witnessed the initial impact and subsequent achievements of several design leaders there firsthand. I had worked closely with each of these leaders and supported them while they transitioned into the organisation. If you do not take the opportunity to discover the past, then you are missing out on a treasure trove of resources and ideas. I was able to keep proven, successful approaches while introducing (and testing) my own new strategies where I could see there were gaps and inefficiencies.

The Solution

Understanding what went before should always be a priority when starting your design leadership role, especially if you are joining a new business which you are unfamiliar with. Before embarking on your new plan of action, take a bit of time to familiarise yourself with the history of the team.

When starting your role, you will be entering one of the following scenarios:

1. The previous leader performed at a low, medium or high level and then moved on to another organisation.
2. The previous leader performed highly and was promoted to the next level in the same company (your role might now report to your predecessor).

Scenario one

In scenario one, you will need to try and discover what really happened in the past – the good and the bad. The tricky part is getting an objective view. The previous leadership style will probably be ingrained in the behaviours of the team, and there may still be employees loyal to your predecessor.

Spend time with each team member to hear their opinions on previous design approaches and to gather a variety of perspectives. This will help you piece together the reality. Some team members may also have great ideas, overlooked by past leaders, that are just waiting to be capitalised on.

Scenario two

In scenario two, the previous leader is still there, potentially overseeing your work. They may still view their approach as best, and they might therefore strongly advise that you follow that path.

This is when you need to truly understand 'what went before' as you'll need to walk the fine line between honouring the accomplishments and successes of your predecessor (which they can give you direct guidance on) and perceiving where there is room for improvement or missteps that could be corrected. This is politically sensitive, of course, and should be done with tact. You shouldn't be seen to discard the past. Rather, you should build on their previous success by evolving their approach using your own experience and skills. In appreciating and respecting their previous work, you can keep them on side while still making the necessary changes.

Drawing It All Together

When you enter your new role as design leader, keep the good, discard the bad and build the new. Of course, this is easier said than done, but you should make a concerted effort to gather information on how things have been accomplished in the past and where there is room for improvement. In this way, you can avoid previous mistakes in order to accelerate your own progress.

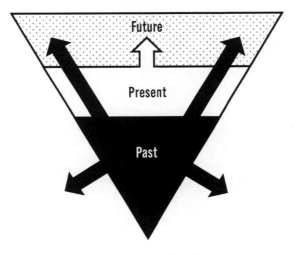

Figure 3.1 The path of understanding what worked before

DESIGN LEAD SUCCEED

4 TRACK YOUR ENVIRONMENT

'The key is to quickly recognise the nature of the threat and then to creatively and expeditiously respond to it. Otherwise, the game will be over before it begins.'

BILL WALSH

What Is the Rule?

The business sector environment in which a company and its products sit – whether geographical, political, social, economic or technological – can have a huge impact on its success or failure, or even its ability to exist. Leading a creative function requires taking part ownership of the organisation's future survival, so you must always be scanning for threats and opportunities. It's essential that you do your own continuous analysis of the organisation's external environment so as to contribute to the creation of the business strategy.

The Problem

The world does not stand still. An organisation's external environment can experience frequent and dramatic shifts due to factors such as natural disasters, actions by governments, financial crises or the release of new technology. These macroeconomic factors, or drivers of change, need to be identified as they emerge and judged whether to be significant or insignificant threats to the future market position and viability of the organisation. For example, consider the COVID-19 pandemic, a macroeconomic factor which influenced change at the microeconomic level of consumer beliefs and behaviours. Many consumers were limited to when and how far they could travel, and they tended to behave in a way which focussed on their mental and physical wellbeing. One of the results of this was a sudden growth in exercising at home, which then drove a high demand for home gym equipment. This was great for gym equipment manufacturers (assuming that their manufacturing and logistics were not too badly affected by the pandemic), but it was not so good for gym owners whose facilities had restricted access at that time.

As the design leader, you need to be acutely aware of changing microeconomic environmental factors such as the beliefs and behaviours of consumers and how that shapes their interaction with businesses, products and services. It is also vital to consider the interplay between the two, i.e. how macroeconomic drivers shape consumer beliefs and therefore behaviours, creating microeconomic trends. The complexity of tracking outside factors that could impact you and your company is hard enough if you only trade within one region or country. If you are creating products for a global audience, the complexity of scanning your external environment becomes compounded because of the need to consider different international and regional cultures, international policies, legal frameworks, behaviours and retail environments.

The Solution

Constant change calls for constant vigilance. You need to be ready to react and prepared to capitalise on any changes that occur so that the products you create remain relevant.

Consider when is best to swot up on the external environment. You'll need to do a fair amount of initial homework when starting the role, but then it's important to continue to stay up-to-date. Plan your schedule to include a regular time slot, perhaps weekly, to research the external environment. This will help you to build clearer predictions for the future. It also helps to keep it relevant and current so it's ready as and when you need to reference it during your daily routine. If you don't have the time, then you could share this work with your team or hire a consultant to help you define and monitor future trends.

Where to find out this information? Read leading industry journals and visit conferences and trade shows. Visit the retailers and speak to the staff. Ask industry experts. If you're already in the role, harvest ideas and opinions from your team.

Gathering your research is important, but so is a methodology for analysis. The combination of three common business frameworks – PEST, SWOT and Porter's Five Forces – work well to distil the core macroeconomic and microeconomic factors affecting your organisation and design function. Each one also provides a visual output which makes the key findings easier to absorb.

PEST is an acronym for political, economic, social and technological factors. It defines the key groups of macroeconomic factors impacting a business.

SWOT is a framework that helps us to analyse a business's competitive position. It's an acronym for strengths, weaknesses, opportunities and threats. In analysing an organisation's opportunities and threats, we can define external environmental factors that might impact the business.

Porter's Five Forces framework then serves as an excellent lens through which to further break down and categorise the external environmental factors affecting an organisation. In Michael Porter's seminal work, he argues that in order for organisations to compete within their marketplace, they have a choice between the three strategies of 'cost leadership – becoming the lowest cost producer in the market', 'differentiation – offering something different, extra, or special', and 'focus – achieving dominance in a niche market'. Whichever strategy or combination of strategies an organisation chooses to follow at a particular time, Porter states that it needs to take into account the following five competitive forces which drive the strategy:

1. Industry competitors – Rivalry among existing firms.
2. Potential entrants – Threat of new entrants (e.g. new business start-ups or businesses from other industries).
3. Buyers – Bargaining power of buyers (e.g. business-to-business (B2B) or direct-to-consumer (D2C)).
4. Substitutes – Threat of substitute products or services (e.g. offering the same/similar functionality as your product).
5. Suppliers – Bargaining power of suppliers (e.g. factories may threaten to increase the prices of the products they supply to companies).

I find that layering this framework over the opportunities and threats categories of the SWOT analysis (See Figure 4.1) allows for a clear unpacking of the external situation of the business. Delving into each area further allows the design-related factors to be identified for more detailed discussion and analysis.

It's always worth trying to define a forecasted time period for the opportunities and threats which you discover. This may involve categorisation into short, medium or long-term, which can aid prioritisation of any planned actions. For instance, there may be many immediate opportunities and threats, but some may emerge at set times when new rules and legislation come into being or at a time when a long-discussed technology from a scientific breakthrough is predicted to occur. Let's explore these factors in more detail, including relevant subcategories, pertinent issues and how to research them further.

Strengths	**Weaknesses**
Opportunities	**Threats**
1. Competitive Rivalry	1. Competitive Rivalry
2. Threat of New Entrants	2. Threat of New Entrants
3. Buyer Power	3. Buyer Power
4. Threat of Substitution	4. Threat of Substitution
5. Supplier Power	5. Supplier Power

Figure 4.1 Porter's Five Forces layered over the opportunities
and threats categories of a SWOT analysis

1. Industry competitors – Rivalry among existing firms

● What are your competitors currently doing, and what are they planning? Do they have new product ranges in the works that could rival yours?

● Build a predicted brand positioning map of all your competitors to visually assess the threat level to your market.

● Download and assess the publicly available corporate planning and annual financial accounts of your competitors to gain insights and clues to their business strategy and future movements.

2. Potential entrants – Threat of new entrants

● You can track new competition at tradeshows and exhibitions and on retail visits.

● Remember that the competitors you identified at the start of your new product development project may be different once you come to launch your product, or there may even be more of them.

3. Buyers – Bargaining power of buyers

● Identify all of your 'buyers' and their attitudes to market trends. Depending on your business model, these could include Amazon, Tmall or the shoppers and consumers buying your product online and in-store.

● Review the biggest trends in your industry for the current year and those predicted for the next five years.

● Consider how cultural developments and preferences might evolve over time.

● Consider shopper design psychology, i.e. the target consumer in your market and how they tend to make a purchasing decision.

● Consider who the biggest influencers are within the industry in terms of consumers and how that might be changing over time. This includes assessment of social media influence and influencers.

4. Substitutes – Threat of substitute products or services

● Keep up-to-date with design industry software and hardware technologies.

● Look at new patents, i.e. who's the most prolific developer/inventor in the industry?

● Track the status of international quality standards such as ISO.

● Stay informed on the global design industry by regularly checking news websites, weekly industry publications and podcasts.

● Colleagues within the business will be additional sources of external news and links.

● Keep track of design associations and awards.

● Be active on LinkedIn and any relevant groups and forums, including those on social media.

5. Suppliers – Bargaining power of suppliers

● Keep track of key influential factors such as raw material prices, material supply, the labour market and trade tariffs between countries.

● Keep an eye on what new materials are emerging which could revolutionise the industry and provide new functionality and performance improvements to products.

Once you have a comprehensive list of threats and opportunities, you then need to prioritise them.

Drawing It All Together

If you have a good grasp of your external environment, you will be strongly positioned to judge the status of a business and the function you are joining. You'll also have clear opinions which will help you to contribute to the business strategy.

You need to be prepared for when the owner or CEO makes an impromptu visit to the design office and asks you for your thoughts. Even if they don't, this research means you are able to more effectively integrate and communicate with colleagues and you can offer an informed opinion on what opportunities could be explored at any given moment. Giving an opinion is one thing, but backing it up with evidence is much more powerful.

More than making your mark among the leadership though, this anticipation of future threats and opportunities is vital to the survival of your company. This is the mindset you need to adopt if you are to stay engaged and lead successfully. Like a tribal scout surveying the landscape and conditions, you need to use all of your senses to pick up tracks and clues. This is the vital information that could determine your next best move. Never let your guard drop. Never forget to check what is happening in the retail space of your fiercest competitors.

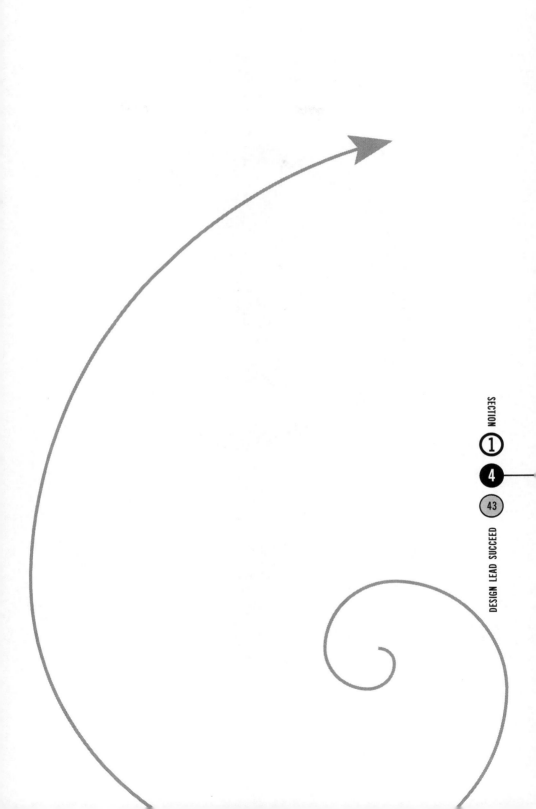

SECTION

HOW TO DEVELOP A POWERFUL MISSION AND ETHOS

How can you mobilise creative individuals and unite them as a team in pursuit of a shared mission which they genuinely believe in and would move mountains to achieve? It's not enough to simply pay people and expect they'll deliver great design work. Only 100% commitment from you will translate into the authentic leadership necessary to build a crystal-clear vision of the future. If you can do this while treating your people well and caring about their continued development, it'll result in a hive of creativity with unstoppable momentum.

These four rules below will help you to develop and share this compelling mission and group ethos to build a strong foundation for success.

5 PUT PEOPLE FIRST

'Treat others as you would like to be treated – with concern and care.'

LOU HOLTZ

What Is the Rule?

Solving the toughest challenges and creating beautiful products, while having fun in the process, requires a highly driven and motivated team with a burning desire to transform the status quo. Unlocking this potential drive and motivation begins with your mindset towards them and then your action of putting your people first on every occasion.

The Problem

If the people in your team are not engaged and passionate about the creative journey, then you have a tough job on your hands. A machine can be controlled at will by an on/off switch, but people are not machines (well, except for a few outstanding individuals I have had the pleasure of working with). People are arguably an organisation's most difficult asset to manage, but they are also the most valuable. They are the only resource that can create value. However, the level of creative value they contribute is directly related to how you choose to treat and lead them. The difference in contribution between high-performing individuals and low-performing individuals can be considerable, so your organisation's productivity relies on you helping them all to reach their potential. Even small gestures and actions can matter significantly to individuals within your care. One example is when an employee has to follow up on holiday requests, even after patiently waiting for weeks for approval. This situation can leave them feeling disheartened and uncertain about their value to the team in the eyes of their boss. So, you need to remember that the quality of project outcomes will depend upon the passion, dedication and loyalty that your team decides to commit, and that, in turn, can depend on how you interact with them.

The Solution

As a leader, you have the power to influence situations for the better. I find a highly effective method of influencing productivity is by always putting your people first. 'People first' is not just a statement but an action! This simple but powerful approach can alter the dynamic of the relationships you have with your team.

By putting an employee first, you are fulfilling a couple of core human needs for them. The need for connection and the need to feel significant. It makes us feel heard and appreciated. When people feel this, they become happier, more confident, loyal and willing to give back in kind through dedication to their work.

But how can we put people first in practice? Consider the following actions, which help to prioritise your employees' needs:

Timing – As team leader, and with people directly reporting to you, start by reacting immediately to any requests and questions that they may have on a daily basis. If the request can be completed in a few minutes, do it immediately. If it will take longer, immediately respond to the individual, acknowledge their request and confirm when they'll receive a result; then complete this within 24 hours. Be consistent in this approach. Consistency builds trust and loyalty. Reply to that email immediately rather than flagging it for later and sign that holiday request on the same day so they can start to make plans. This sends the message that you value them and that they are important.

Decision-making – Prioritise the wellbeing of your organisation's people in any decision that you have to make. For example, if there is work that needs to be completed urgently, consider how to avoid asking them to come in on the weekend; instead, get them involved in a more creative solution. Another example would be when considering a change of office and seating configuration for your team. Include the individuals in the decision-making process and allow them as much choice as possible in the set-up and configuration of their working space because it will impact their mental health and productivity.

Consistency – Putting your employees first once is not enough. You need to build trust and acceptance by being consistent with your repeated actions of support.

Workload – Do not offload jobs onto individuals without discussing the work with them and finding out if they feel they have the necessary capabilities, tools, support and available time. Care about their workload and take the time to understand if it's manageable.

Approach – Treat people as unique human beings first rather than generic employees. By giving them attention and care, you are valuing them as whole people and not just worker bees.

Regular contact – Give them time to talk to you and listen intently to them. Set aside specific meeting times for direct reports each week where you can discuss ongoing work and what is going on in their world. It helps to steer and resolve issues early on before bigger problems build up through miscommunication.

Focus on the positives – Always try to see the good in people. We can't always get along with everyone, and certain personalities don't always combine well. But try to push this to one side and, as a leader, look for the aspects in their character that you like and value.

Self-awareness – Do not forget that your own mood and demeanour have a big effect on the mood of the team. If you are stressed and agitated, then this could transfer to them. Try to contain and control your emotions so as not to disrupt the performance of your team or the atmosphere in the office.

Let go of your insecurities – Let go of your personal disappointment when people eventually decide to move on and take the next step in their career. Be happy for them if they decide to leave and, hopefully, they will become an ambassador for your company. They may even return one day if they've had a great experience.

Anticipate – Work on developing your skills of empathy and sensitivity. Learn to get a 'feel' for a situation and anticipate when 'people first' situations arise. It's not always obvious when it's needed. For example, an employee may be battling on when they are overloaded with work and struggling mentally, afraid to let you down or show weakness. If you don't catch this early, you may lose the employee altogether once they get to the stage of burnout.

Drawing It All Together

Small things matter in the way you interact with your team. Putting people first can make a big difference to an individual's performance, but it is also the right thing to do. Even if they eventually leave your team, and they will, they may become advocates for you and your organisation. Word of mouth and low turnover of staff will help to build a reputation. People will want to join your team and be part of your creative journey. This is why it's essential to treat people as the most important part of the organisation and make their personal wellbeing and development your highest priority. If you look after your people, they will look after you and the projects.

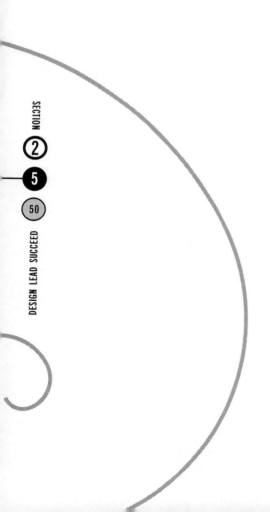

6 NURTURE A POSITIVE AND CREATIVE CULTURE

'Culture eats strategy for breakfast.'

PETER DRUCKER

What Is the Rule?

Culture is arguably the most powerful but often the most forgotten force at play within a business. From day one, a culture exists within your business or team. However, it evolves and, most importantly, it can be harnessed. In terms of productivity, it can be the difference between swimming with the tide or against it. Creative culture often forms as a result of the influential structures put in place by the company founder and the original leadership team, such as mission statements, founding stories and values which promote creativity and innovation. These are then embedded by formal and informal daily communications and interactions between employees, whether it's meetings, chats in the corridor, emails or lunchtime breaks together. The leader of a start-up business will have control and influence over the culture they wish to develop from its inception. However, if the business is long-established, the culture is inherited, and its suitability for nurturing success therefore needs to be assessed.

The Problem

Culture is like personality. It's unique to that individual or business. It can be destructive or it can be energising and motivational. Recognise that culture has momentum. Once it has taken root in one particular form, it can be difficult to change course. As a leader, you can create and drive a positive culture, but you must also try to turn around a negative one. I have experienced the power of cultural momentum in an organisation when the ingredients have been right. The CEO was immersed in the business and the industry that we operated in. Their dedication and commitment to the cause was inspiring and infectious. Every time they spoke to the group, their passion and belief permeated. They could create goose bumps. They were authentic! This proved to me the power of the contribution a leader could make to building an organisation's culture. And this wasn't just another charismatic leader using their personality to evoke emotion. They worked hard to implement formal foundations that allowed the culture to thrive, shaping business purpose, strategies and the leadership team around a central goal. Every monthly business update from the CEO felt like a motivational team talk which engaged every employee. They reiterated the purpose, mission and key strategies in very simple terms which everyone in the organisation could understand. There was stability in the culture and commitment to the mission.

However, the problem goes beyond implementing a successful culture. Businesses must evolve regularly in order to adjust to the ever-changing needs of their shoppers, consumers, customers and industry. But the culture of a successful company takes time to develop and become embedded. At a certain point, critical mass is achieved, and the balance of employees are influenced for long enough that they take on, use and evolve shared rituals

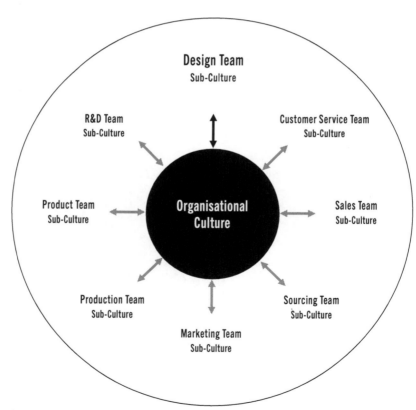

Figure 6.1 The interplay between organisational culture and team sub-cultures

and behaviours which contribute to the performance of the organisation. However, this is where the difficulty occurs. If businesses must evolve to better serve their consumers and the market, then a successful culture is destabilised. As the design function is a sub-culture of the larger organisational culture (a smaller tribe) as outlined in Figure 6.1, any problems with the wider organisational culture will inevitably affect them too.

As an example, the leadership team of a business may initiate organisational restructures to meet the changing needs of the consumer and industry. They may do this with the best of intentions but, critically, their employees have become the living embodiment of the culture. When groups of people are removed, or enough of them are alienated, the culture that once existed begins to diminish and deteriorate. But avoiding change altogether, or even making the incorrect change, could result in bankruptcy. It's a tricky balance.

The Solution

Culture is a powerful driving force. You should consider how it can be shaped, maintained and harnessed to boost creative productivity.

In order to do this, it is important to consider the factors which can nurture a company's creative culture – whether they are informal factors that merely influence in order to nudge it in the right direction or more formal, directive factors that support concrete change and shape employee behaviour. Figure 6.2 suggests many of the cultural factors at play. These factors are grouped as either 'core' or 'supporting'. Core factors help set the 'creative culture' dimension of the organisation. These might include stories of how the organisation was founded and the mission statement. Nike is a great example of a highly creative and innovative organisation whose mission statement is to 'bring inspiration and innovation to every athlete* in the world (*If you have a body, you are an athlete)'. This is a call to action which defines a goal and gives every employee the permission to fulfil it. Creativity is woven into the founding stories of Nike as Bill Bowerman, a track and field coach and one of the cofounders, experimented in his garage with different materials to create many of the company's early running shoe outsole innovations.

But how does this relate to the design team? As the design leader, you are a major factor shaping the design sub-culture. If your role is also to be part of the company leadership team, you will have a strong influence on the overall organisational culture. This means you are uniquely positioned to become the catalyst for establishing or maintaining a 'creative culture'. In this role, you should encourage a focus on and respect for design creation

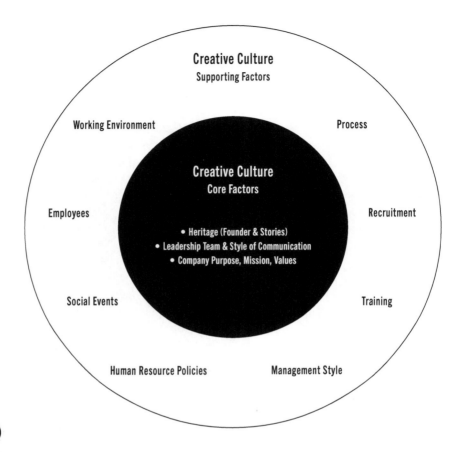

Figure 6.2 Contributing factors to a creative culture

in the organisation's leadership, as well as an appreciation of the value that it can bring to performance.

Let's look again at the core and supporting factors that shape a creative culture, outlined in Figure 6.2, and how you can approach each one as a design leader:

Heritage – Founder and stories (core factor)

● Was the founder of the company a creative? If so, this fact in itself, as well as their creative spirit, their story of struggle and their eventual success, should be embraced and shared regularly with the design team as an example to emulate.

● Utilise design success stories from the organisation's past to motivate your team and the company. Focus on the role of design in its achievements. For example, if it's relevant, you could highlight how design and innovation revolutionised the product and industry at that time. Over time, the stories will permeate through the organisation. They can also be shared externally, reinforcing the creative credentials and pedigree of the brand with the consumer by building greater awareness, loyalty and perceived quality.

Leadership team and style of communication (core factor)

• Can the leadership team evolve its style of communication to inspire and motivate? For example, how does it deal with risk? Does it encourage employees to try new things or does it hamper their creativity? Does it invest in design and innovation teams and initiatives sufficiently? Does it give the teams the strength and depth to explore and experiment in order to attain the key insights necessary to help build paradigm-shifting technologies and products?

• The position of a 'chief design officer' or equivalent on the senior leadership team of an organisation serves as a symbol of commitment to creativity. This should be an individual with a creative background and technical knowhow who can influence the business strategy. They should be able to promote creative ways of working and utilise the value which design and innovation can offer, which will ultimately deliver greater commercial returns for the business.

• Look at setting up systems of reward for teams and individuals that demonstrate company values and deliver results through creative methods. Some companies provide financial incentives for generating assets such as new patented inventions, for instance.

• In-house competitions to build solutions are another way to help motivate teams, with the winning solution going forward to production. This approach is more feasible in larger organisations which have multiple design teams based across different sites and countries.

• Can you encourage the leadership team to discuss, share and promote their desire to produce products which are renowned for their aesthetic appeal and not just cheap to manufacture? This will encourage all members of the organisation to adopt this more creative mindset.

Company purpose, mission and values (core factor)

• The 'purpose statement' of an organisation defines why it exists. Great purpose statements are highly motivating calls to action and in some way contribute towards the greater good of all mankind and the planet. For example, Patagonia's purpose statement is: 'We're in business to save our home planet'. Arguably, people join an organisation because they are attracted to the brand and its purpose and mission or they have an affinity for the founder of the business. This helps to build an organisation of like-minded individuals who will generate a positive culture with a forward momentum.

- The 'mission statement' of an organisation defines what it does and for whom, and this is exactly what the previous Nike example did with its aim to 'bring inspiration and innovation to every athlete* in the world'. The words 'inspiration' and 'innovation' clearly define the level of expected product quality needed by the consumer. This statement thus serves as a creative stretch objective for the whole organisation.
- But what if there is no reference to creativity or innovation within the purpose or mission statement of your organisation and you're unable to change it? You can always define a design-specific mission statement which aligns with the organisation's existing statements. This can break down the action statement to include creative actions which are more tangible and relevant to the creation of the products you're building. This approach aids in developing a creative culture because the design team feel a clearer connection between what they do and the aims of the organisation.

Working environment (supporting factor)
- Consider creating spaces for more informal and off-the-cuff meetings and chats over coffee. This helps support more natural interaction between employees when it's needed rather than when it's scheduled.
- Adorn the walls with past art and design works so as to immerse employees in the visual identity of the company and celebrate its successes.
- Include pictures of the founder and stories about their journey in the entrance space so it is the first and last thing that staff and visitors see each day as a reminder of the company's mission and purpose.

Employees (supporting factor)
- Poor staff attitudes and behaviours can spread like a virus throughout a team and organisation. Identify toxic individuals and set out standards for them to meet in order to change their behaviour before removing them from the organisation.
- Identify your longest-serving and most loyal staff and keep them close and embedded in the organisation as advocates. Positive and established employees act as guardians of the culture: their knowledge, rituals and behaviours are of great value in maintaining it. But if cultural change is needed, they can also be barriers depending on the individuals. In these instances, seek out these key team members and listen to their concerns to bring them onboard.

Recruitment (supporting factor)
- Many of the most successful companies and design teams throughout the world have a strong, distinctive culture which attracts applicants

and reflects the personality of the products and services they create. Building a great culture can thus be critical to successful recruitment.

• When you're hiring people, it's important to consider whether they will fit the culture of the current business and help to build it. Their skills alone are not enough. Do they wish to join for the right reasons, and are they enthused by the mission?

• Wherever possible, minimise making too many team member changes at any one time, or you'll seriously damage the established culture. If it's currently thriving, this could be a huge risk to your future success.

Process (supporting factor)
• Process can serve as an invaluable method for forming a common creative culture. By defining a product development process for the entire organisation, this becomes a formal and agreed working protocol which can help to direct behaviour and decision-making in ways which align with company values.

Training (supporting factor)
• On-the-job training is an excellent opportunity to grow and reinforce the creative culture by sharing the best behaviours, design skills and knowledge between individuals within the team and wider organisation.

• Tailored group training schemes are also a good opportunity to develop a shared creative culture. The tailored approach means that individuals within the organisation are taught the same learning material, which can help to align ways of thinking and approaches to problem-solving.

Human resource policies (supporting factor)
• As the key point of communication between the organisation and the senior management team or business owner, it's vital that the human resources team helps to instil the desired culture. They should support and reflect the behaviours and approaches laid out by the leadership team in their policies. The culture should also be expressed in the way they communicate and interact with employees. HR professionals should consider the following issues in order to create a positive culture:

- Hours of work: For creative activities, people should not be chained to their desks for a certain number of hours. There should be flexibility that respects the creative process.
- Employee wellbeing: People's health and happiness should be prioritised in policies and in interactions.
- Inclusivity: A culture of inclusivity is important and should be nurtured

to ensure everyone can bring their best self to work. This should be supported by robust policies.

– Rewarding integrity: The company should make a point of formally and informally rewarding honesty, integrity and loyalty in their employees.

Management style (supporting factor)

• Your style of leadership sets the tone for the energy and engagement of a design department. The team's feelings can hinge on your own mood, attitude and the presence which you project. Always try to manage your emotions and stay calm and level-headed. This has a big impact on their happiness and output.

• Your company culture and the sub-culture you choose to create must have the ability to adapt as the situation evolves. By building a company culture from day one which accepts continuous change, you are creating resilience, flexibility and positivity in the face of uncertainty.

• Try to manage culture as another ongoing project. It's something that always requires your attention, care and time.

• Minimise your micro-management of the team, giving them space and time for experimentation. This will give them the chance to grow and will encourage them to remain with you for the long-term. Try not to blame them for their mistakes. Focus on the situation and how that could be changed to create a more productive context in which they can succeed. This will lead to a more engaged team who are more highly skilled individuals at the end of the project. As a leader, you'll also benefit from feeling more secure and confident that the important tasks are being attended to.

• Lead by example and don't be afraid to do the basic, dirty jobs that you ask your team to do. It sounds obvious, but showing them that you're prepared to do this demonstrates that no type of work is below anybody.

• Try to speak to individuals in a way that motivates them. A parental manner of communication is the tendency to talk down to people as a parent might give instruction to a child. This style can feel patronising and belittling. If you give them respect and avoid negativity and public shaming, they will be more relaxed and confident – the perfect conditions for maximum creativity. If you're interested in reading more about this, take a look at transactional analysis theory.

• Be consistent and set transparent parameters. For example, you need to set clear boundaries for expected performance and behaviours and avoid changing the rules so employees know what you want from them. This builds trust and creates a stable environment so the team won't be on edge.

Social events (supporting factor)

- Regular team lunches help to galvanise relationships among individuals. This can aid project work collaboration and build ongoing rapport.
- Planning in the space and time for the design team to celebrate after key team calendar milestones or after major projects, either through nights out or trips away, is a great way to bring the design team together and build motivation for the next challenge.
- Free meals and even a full-time free canteen can help in significantly boosting morale and pulling even the quieter individuals away from their working spaces for periods of social interaction, idea sharing and friendship building.

Drawing It All Together

In summary, a positive culture is crucial to success. Don't ignore the need to nurture your team and organisational culture in order to draw in and retain the right people. Realise its potential and the huge contribution it can make. It can be a great driving force to aid creativity and design.

Recognise that there are a huge variety of elements that contribute to building company culture, some of which are easy to control and some of which are more ephemeral and difficult to influence.

For a company's creative culture to support maximum creativity, it should be supportive of the creative process and respect the individuals tasked with carrying out these activities.

7 MAKE THE MISSION CLEAR AND GET THE TEAM ONBOARD

'A shared vision is not an idea . . . it is, rather, a force in people's hearts . . . at its simplest level, a shared vision is the answer to the question "What do we want to create?"'

PETER SENGE

What Is the Rule?

As the design leader, you must ensure that everyone in your team understands the mission – the business's overall purpose and strategy. Every member of the team should grasp how their individual creative contributions must combine to help deliver the design team's objectives and, ultimately, the business objectives. If they are all working towards a common goal, you can focus their creative energy on building something valuable.

The Problem

Creativity is essential for an organisation wishing to develop original ideas that evolve into innovative solutions. But without effective management, an abundance of creativity can lead to a lack of business focus and possible inertia. For example, you may generate lots of great opportunities for different projects, but by pursuing too many of these projects at one time, you'll slow your progress overall, and it may lead to project cancellations and disillusionment if tangible results are not proven and market-ready in time. In most companies, there are finite resources available, so effective management means clear prioritisation and committing those resources to the few projects which are most focussed on delivering the organisation's strategic objectives. For creativity to build successful outcomes, it needs to be aligned with the organisation's purpose and directed towards the organisation's objectives in this way. Quite often, the purpose comes from the business founder's or senior management's original vision, and the organisation's purpose, vision and mission statements clearly define why the organisation exists and how it intends to achieve its objectives. These objectives are then set out in the business strategy, a coordinated plan that explains how they'll be achieved on an annual or long-term basis.

It's vital that an organisation has a clear understanding of where it's going – a mission – otherwise it can easily get lost along the way. Without this, you and your design team will be confused as to how best to channel your ideas and energy. You'll experience the constant challenge of trying to effectively manage a diverse group of creative individuals who have no unified direction. By its very nature, creativity is a process of divergence with multiple ideas and possibilities open for exploration. But this is then followed by a period of convergence towards a chosen solution through various methods of evaluation. Without a purpose to guide you, there is no way of driving that process to produce a final idea that meets the criteria. The importance of a clear company purpose is supported by a Deloitte research project whose findings identified that purpose-driven companies experience higher productivity, growth rates that are three times faster on average than competitors and more satisfied staff who choose to remain with the organisation for longer. They also found that these companies experienced 30% higher levels of innovation.

The Solution

There should always be a clear purpose, vision and mission statement that everyone can get behind and which drives the business strategy. For example, the purpose of Adidas is: 'Through sport we have the power to change lives', which helps to guide the way that Adidas is operated. Their mission is also stated as: 'To be the best sports brand in the world'. Regardless of an organisation's size, those elements must be clear and understood by everyone. It's your job as the design leader to ensure that everyone in your team grasps how they can contribute as individuals. Figure 7.1 shows how the business strategy of an organisation connects with the purpose, vision and mission statement guiding the annual strategic objectives.

As a design leader, I've found a number of different approaches which have been effective in communicating and executing business strategy:

Remind them regularly

I've always found that it's important to clearly communicate the business strategy to the team on a regular basis because it builds their familiarity with it as well as their confidence, faith and focus on the direction that

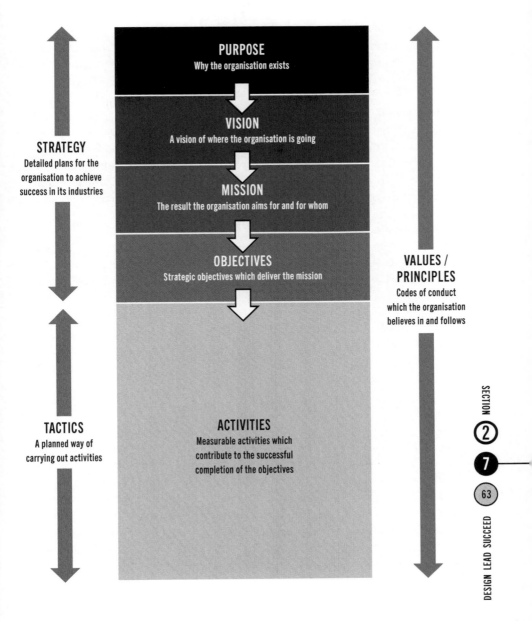

PURPOSE
Why the organisation exists

VISION
A vision of where the organisation is going

MISSION
The result the organisation aims for and for whom

OBJECTIVES
Strategic objectives which deliver the mission

ACTIVITIES
Measurable activities which
contribute to the successful
completion of the objectives

STRATEGY
Detailed plans for the
organisation to achieve
success in its industries

TACTICS
A planned way of
carrying out activities

**VALUES /
PRINCIPLES**
Codes of conduct
which the organisation
believes in and follows

Figure 7.1 Components of the business strategy

the organisation is taking. This can be done in monthly or quarterly team design meetings where you review team progress against specific design business objectives.

Get them involved

Encourage input and feedback from the team regarding the business strategy and the proposed design activities. This helps to strengthen the approach and build individual buy-in and commitment to the cause.

Break it down

Take the organisation's business strategy and break it down into the desired tactics and activities of the team and individuals so as to produce a clear plan of action. At the end of this there should be a design team document which can be shared physically and digitally. This helps to visually show a direct line of connection between the strategy and individuals' actions.

Make it specific to the design team

If the strategy or purpose statement is not specific enough to the design team, break it down and make it more relevant and product focussed. Create a design-specific statement which defines the products you're building. In tailoring the corporate message to your team and their day-to-day activities, you will build their motivation and ownership, galvanising them towards a common goal.

Drawing It All Together

With a strong purpose statement and business strategy for the organisation and design team to follow, the rest of your creative journey should be properly focused, and things will be more likely to fall into place. They will help you make clear and well-founded decisions about anything you do. If the possible outcome of a decision doesn't align with your purpose and strategy, then it needs to be questioned! Effectively managing and communicating your purpose and strategy to your design team will set a great foundation from which to build the rest of your leadership responsibilities.

8 SET SHARED PRINCIPLES

'Principles drive values and goals and act as anchors during difficult and conflicting times.'

GEORGE A. GOENS

What Is the Rule?

Exceptional design is the result of high-performing teams, and so you are looking to nurture a sense of cohesion and solidarity. Setting shared team principles which are anchored to your organisational values will bring together individuals who might normally clash. They serve as actionable rules around behaviour and approach, and they help to maintain high levels of focus, harmony and collaboration.

The Problem

Teams have the potential to compete internally and ultimately unravel if left unchecked. Design can be a subjective discipline to manage, and disagreements can arise about standards and approaches. At times, people can also be emotionally driven by conflicting personal values and agendas. The creative potential of a team arises in part from the diversity of the individuals within it – their different backgrounds, knowledge, skills and personalities – but how do you maintain focus, harmony and collaboration given these differences?

The Solution

If you want a high-performing team – incorporating trust, collaboration, openness and all of the other attributes which contribute to maximum creativity and productivity – then you need a solution which helps to unite individuals regardless of their diversity and the size of the team. It's incorrect to assume that people will naturally behave in the same way and make the same decisions as you would as their leader. They'll probably have different experience to you, in terms of technical skills and communication, as well as different mindsets and values. You therefore need a method of setting and maintaining a level of appropriate behaviour as well as a required performance level in their design execution.

Creating a set of shared principles is a solution to this problem as it will help to steer their behaviour and interactions to create an environment ripe for maximum creativity. By shared principles, I mean accepted rules or a code of conduct for the group. Many larger organisations already have a set of corporate principles or values (normally located in their business strategy document) which are usually top-level and overarching in order to remain relevant to every employee, regardless of their function. However, in my experience, they're not as powerful and impactful as building those principles at a team level. However, the overarching business values could be used as a foundation from which to build more detailed and relevant design-specific principles relating to their day-to-day roles.

Here are a few suggestions as to how to set up these design-specific principles:

Consider values versus principles

The terms 'values' and 'principles' are similar in meaning, regularly used interchangeably and often confused. But I believe it's important to try and make a distinction between them for clarity. In my opinion, 'values' define the worth or importance of something. They are intangible until acted out in the behaviour and decisions of a business or individual. Many people don't even know what their personal values are and what lies beneath them, even though they may influence every decision and action they take. Figure 8.1 visualises how the values of employees and the business they work for may vary. This is the norm. Although some people are naturally drawn to businesses that align with their personal values, the business may not share all of them. Individuals may be further away or closer to the values of the business as shown in the figure.

'Principles', on the other hand, are anchored on values, but they are articulated as actionable rules. I prefer the definition of principles as rules, codes of conduct or the underlying workings of an entity. Figure 8.2 shows an example of how design team principles can remain aligned to business values but can also act as clear guard rails for employee conduct.

Shared ownership

Build the list of principles with your team. You can steer the process from the start with suggestions and ideas and make the final decision if it's

Figure 8.1 – Comparing the values of a business against its employees

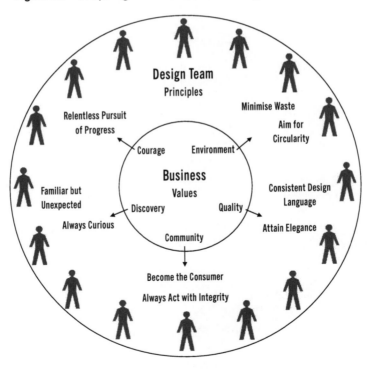

Figure 8.2 – Alignment of design team principles with business values

not obvious what should stay and what should go. However, it's vitally important that the team buys into these shared principles, so the whole process of creating them should be inclusive.

Find sources of inspiration

When putting together your principles, do your research. Begin by looking to successful design teams, businesses and people and how they behave, interact, communicate and approach design work. For example, Dieter Rams' *Ten Principles for Good Design* provides an excellent starting point because these design-specific principles are fairly universal and have stood the test of time. They can provide you with inspiration as to how to collaborate most effectively.

Choosing the topics

Try to find a good balance between design execution principles, which will help to guide the 'how' and 'what' of the design, with behavioural principles, which will help to guide how individuals should interact in relation to team communication, prioritisation, creativity and design decision-making. Warren Buffet mentions his core values of energy, intelligence and integrity when looking for new recruits to his business. All of your principles could sit within one of these three categories. This is what I do to great effect with my own design teams.

Keep it short and sweet

I've found the rule is 'the simpler, the better' when it comes to shared principles, so that people can remember them easily. I've always tried to define less than 10.

Living the principles

Lead by example and try to embody the set of shared principles in your everyday work. If you slip up, that's fine, but you should hold up your hand, take ownership and declare that you will try to improve. The principles also need to be regularly reaffirmed, perhaps at team meetings, and posted in clear sight on the studio walls to ensure they are fresh in your team's minds and not just left in a dusty folder on a shelf.

Flexibility

The shared principles will take time to embed and test. If a principle is not serving your end goals in the way you expected during this time, there should be flexibility to modify or rewrite it. This is the only way to ensure it remains useful and robust.

After I implemented shared principles within my design team, I found that I was regularly referring to them, and so were the team. This meant we could all hold each other accountable when our behaviour veered off course. And because we had all agreed to the principles, it only required a quick check-in to agree that we should modify our actions. There was no long and drawn-out argument over who was right or wrong or what we should do next. It became a more indirect and diplomatic way of challenging and correcting behaviours. I also found the principles useful for recruiting because they would concisely explain the culture of the team and what we all expected of new hires.

Drawing It All Together

Values underpin the purpose of a business. However, values are not as effective as action-orientated principles in helping to define the collective design approach and behaviour of the design team.

Creativity benefits from a diversity of ideas and backgrounds, and a variety of opinions creates healthy debate. However, conflict can occasionally arise from this diversity, which is not ideal for team rapport and performance if it's allowed to escalate or go unresolved. It's in these situations where shared principles become invaluable guard rails to keep each other in check. If the principles have been agreed by the group, then each person has permission to challenge another member if they feel they're not living up to them. This can help to de-escalate conflict by swiftly and objectively reframing the situation back to the business purpose, vision and mission. A high-performing team is then able to maintain its momentum and trajectory towards exceptional design work.

SECTION

HOW TO CURATE AND LEAD YOUR A TEAM

You can't succeed on your own! But you won't succeed with a team either unless you bring the right group of people together and you're able to stop negative behaviours from derailing the creative process. Creative activity needs to be channelled correctly. As design leader, you'll need to establish clear role remits to allow strong interpersonal relationships to blossom and become the catalyst for creative synergy.

The rules in this section of the book will equip you with the skills to build and lead your A team.

9 ELIMINATE EGOS

'A discussion should be a genuine attempt to explore a subject rather than a battle between competing egos.'

EDWARD DE BONO

What Is the Rule?

Ultimately, you want the best ideas to prevail in any discussion. When leading a group of creative individuals, it's important to recognise that everyone has an ego which is unique to them, and it's in constant adjustment depending on their perception of the situation at that moment in time. Our egos have the potential to disrupt a discussion to serve our needs and desires rather than the needs of the group, the organisation, the design challenge and the user. So, as the leader, you need to be consciously aware of this issue, understanding how the ego manifests and then taking corrective action to defuse the situation. But, more importantly, you need to create an environment where egos are managed.

The Problem

Some people are naturally more egocentric, ignoring the bigger picture and prioritising their individual needs and personal agendas above the project, the team and the business. These individuals become protective of their work, information and responsibilities, which results in them being less open-minded and pushing back against suggestions and design direction. If left unchecked, the ego of individuals can stifle the creativity of the design team and derail projects by damaging team culture and relationships through breakdowns in communication and collaboration. This creates friction within the design team, and this friction will often spread more widely to other teams within the business. As the design leader, you should also be conscious of not using your own position to pursue a more personal agenda if you're representing a brand. This is obviously not an issue if you and your name are the brand and it's your company.

The amount of academic literature surrounding the subject of the 'ego' is extensive! The goal of this chapter is not to explore the topic in great detail and depth but merely to raise your awareness of its presence in everyone, its potential impact and how to minimise its detrimental effects. The renowned psychologist Sigmund Freud was the first to suggest the concept of the 'ego' within his three-part model of personality. He suggested that the personality consists of the id, the ego and the superego. These aren't physical aspects but processes within the brain involving the conscious and unconscious mind. The id is the instinctual, biological driver of our personality, whereas the superego reflects our conscience, morality and social aspects. The ego, on the other hand, is the conscious, decision-making aspect of personality which has to reason and rationalise between the conflicting aspects of the id, the superego and the external environment. And it's this aspect of the ego – its continual development and struggle to reconcile and find justification within the world for the individual – that makes it so pivotal to our nature.

The Solution

It's impossible to fully eliminate ego! However, greater awareness of its impact goes a long way to managing any negative impact on yourself and the individuals within your team. In the main, egos which act out in opposition to the team are driven by personal fears. These fears will be unique to that particular individual and their personality, reflecting their situation and future ambitions. As design leader, you won't always witness egos acting out firsthand, but you'll notice the aftermath or hear of the impact that it has had on relationships and the progress of the project. The best approach to minimising the negative impact of ego on your team is to be proactive and build in preventative measures. Devise a working environment and creative approach which helps to mitigate rogue egos by considering how they may act out when various buttons are pushed and they feel fear. It might also be worth considering training sessions with your team around personality traits so that they can better understand their individual pressure points and the impact of ego on their behaviour.

Consider the following leadership approaches to alleviating each of these common fears in order to keep egos in check:

The fear of losing power and creative control

• Outline clear responsibilities and reasonable levels of working autonomy as they will help to alleviate the need to cling onto and hide knowledge.

- Avoid silos and insist on transparency to help remove the space for egos to hide information.
- Give everyone the opportunity to contribute at the start of the project. Copy the full team into the brief once its created.
- Ensure design work is credited to the whole team regardless of who worked on it. This helps to put people at ease because they feel safe. They'll be more relaxed, and they won't feel like they need to compete. They'll also be less emotionally attached to their original ideas and embrace the process of collective generation of iterative ideas towards a 'best' solution.
- Don't take too much credit as leader. When talking about projects, emphasise 'we' rather than 'I'. Give credit to the individuals in the team who have been creating the work when discussing the project with others externally. This builds up their confidence and makes them feel appreciated.
- Regularly restate the mission of the team to reinforce the bigger picture. This reminds them that the work is for the benefit of the business and brand and not the individual.

The fear of making mistakes and being wrong
- Create a working environment where there is less fear of finger-pointing when situations go wrong and mistakes are made. As leader, it helps when you reiterate that you are ultimately held responsible for the outputs of the team.
- Make sure that everyone feels safe and comfortable to express ideas regardless of how abstract and random they may be.
- Encourage openness and allow people to question situations.

The fear of not being liked
- Give regular credit and genuine praise for work carried out and show them appreciation.
- Have fun as a team. Make plans to get together and commit to this time so the team can bond. This could be anything from a team lunch to evening refreshments to a sports activity or a museum visit.

Drawing It All Together

Unblocking the limitations to creativity that ego can create means developing greater awareness of how it shows up in our teams and ourselves; this is the foundation that will help us to better manage its balanced and rational functioning. Ego issues can arise at any time, but they are particularly likely in moments of stress and high emotion. So, it's important to consider the atmosphere you're creating; something that's heavily driven by your own leadership style and demeanour. Contrary to this chapter's title, your goal is not to fully eliminate the ego and its management of the conscious mind, but rather to keep it in check for the good of your team and the business.

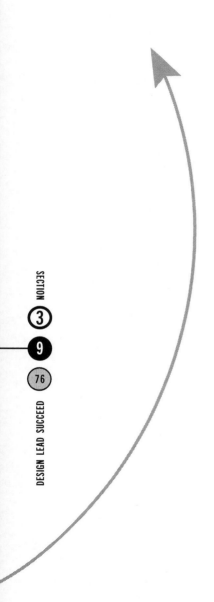

10 BUILD TRUST

'If people like you, they'll listen to you. But if they trust you, they'll do business with you. They will follow you. They will be loyal to you.'

ZIG ZIGLAR

What Is the Rule?

As the design leader, it is critical that you have the full trust of your team, your peers and the company board. Their approval, whether formal or informal, will help to dramatically speed up your progress. Someone originally trusted in you and gave you your leadership role, but that's not enough. Building trust – in yourself, in the products you create and in a brand you develop – begins with you, and it takes an ongoing effort.

The Problem

Without trust from those around you, you won't be able to achieve the things you want to. The quality of the relationship between two individuals or groups is critical for progress in any area of business. Arguably, two of the most important areas where greater trust can accelerate progress in your role will be in the sign-off of funding for utilising design resources and tools and in design approvals at each stage of the design creation process. Let's take the latter as an example. On the journey to creating amazing products, there are many design approvals from different stakeholders along the way. The stakeholders will vary between new and old acquaintances. Often, a great idea, clearly explained with beautiful illustrations, may not be enough to guarantee selection. When predicting the outcome of an idea, stakeholders also consider the designer or the organisation's reputation and track record. Are they credible? Are they reliable? And can they successfully develop the idea through to a final commercial solution? Do they believe you will return the value you promise? Without rapport between the person presenting the idea and the person making the decision, the selection process can be unpredictable.

Trust is important not only for you but also among your team and between your team and others. It helps things to run smoothly. Imagine an engine without enough oil pumping around its many different, interconnecting parts. Heat and friction will increase, and the individual parts will eventually slow and seize up. Trust is like the oil in an engine. With trust, there is greater collaboration and levels of creativity between individuals, speeding up decision-making. For me, it was often clear why design reviews went productively between the design team and stakeholders. Sign-off was based on their proposals successfully meeting the brief, but it was also because strong relationships had developed across departments. Our actions follow our beliefs.

The Solution

Trust is a slippery thing to describe and manufacture, but it's essential. It's organic, subjective and driven by emotion because we are talking about the personally-held opinions and beliefs of individuals. However, by acting in a human way towards others, you can nurture a foundation of mutual good faith.

Here are some possible approaches for building trust that have worked for me:

Make a consistent effort with people – Whether it is with your team, your boss, your client or your friends, make it your daily mission to build trust and rapport. Take an interest in people, ask questions and listen more than you speak. Importantly, be authentic and genuinely care about what the other person is saying. Trust will build through your consistent actions and interactions over a sustained period of time. Do exactly what you say you are going to do and when you said you were going to do it. And do this again and again. Staying true to your values helps you to be consistent because our values are anchored to our authentic self. Our belief in someone is strengthened when we have evidence of past results.

Build the right culture – Trust can flourish more easily within the right culture, and culture is, to a large extent, created and influenced by leaders. As the leader, therefore, you have the power to create an open culture where dishonesty, complaining and finger-pointing are not tolerated.

Trust your team – You can build trust with your team by delegating more and empowering them to make decisions. This is a virtuous circle because if you trust them, they will trust you. Once you have their trust, you can be secure in the knowledge that they'll deliver a great result. Once they have your reassurance, they'll make sure they achieve your objectives.

Understand people's limits – Not everyone you encounter will want to strengthen your mutual connection. Some people will be a closed book. However, where necessary, you may need to manage such relationships without trust being a contributing factor.

Follow up on promises – When agreeing to do something for someone, don't wait for them to check in with you. Follow up with them to confirm that you have done what you agreed to do and demonstrate or show the good results. This helps to remind people that you are trustworthy.

Always be professional – Follow good practice to the letter and do the right thing even when no one is watching. Make your progress visible to everyone so they can see that you can be relied on. For example, clear documentation and planning tools will help to demonstrate your competent management of resources.

You may already be doing all of these things, but how can you tell if someone trusts you? It's obvious in their actions. They ask for your opinion on matters. They recommend you to others. They release funds and provide approval without asking to see all of the details because they have dealt with you in the same situation before and believe that you will do the same good work. They check up on your progress less rigorously because they believe that you'll produce results and meet your deadlines.

Just as you want others to trust you, you want to be able to trust the people in your team. This is another reason why the recruitment process is so important. It's your opportunity to screen individuals to find clues about their past performance and behaviour and potential future performance. References can be checked, but value-based questions during the interview stage can also highlight how trustworthy an individual is.

Drawing It All Together

Trust must be grown and nurtured, which takes time. This puts you at a disadvantage when you're joining a new organisation. In this scenario, you'll need to be scrupulously consistent, professional and back up your words with actions. Finally, remember that trust is difficult and time-consuming to build, so it's vital that you guard it and fight to preserve it by trying not to break promises or miss agreed deadlines. Once trust is broken, it is very difficult to repair the relationship damage it causes and return to the same level of connection.

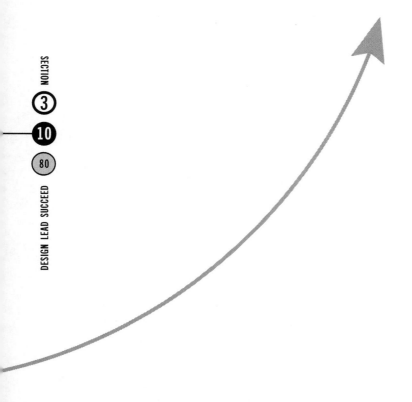

11 ASSEMBLE YOUR A TEAM

'The old adage, "People are your most important asset" is wrong. People are not your most important asset, the right people are.'

JIM COLLINS

What Is the Rule?

People are your greatest resource, and one of your biggest priorities should be finding the right ones to support you in your mission. As a leader, you don't have time to get involved in every activity, and you can't and should not be the star of every skillset. This is why you need to find those key individuals who can excel in their specific areas of expertise, leaving you to coordinate them and chart a course to success. You must search for, identify and secure the best new recruits for your team as swiftly as possible.

DESIGN LEAD SUCCEED

The Problem

Breakthrough products and disruptive innovation cannot emerge without the right calibre of individuals within your team. This underlines the importance of your role as a talent scout. And this isn't just about hiring. Freak events, organisational restructures and individuals' changing circumstances are just some of the many issues that can threaten to destabilise the profile and performance of your team. Someone might move away for personal growth reasons, wanting to experience designing within another agency or create their own design agency so they can be their own boss. You're always at risk of having your most talented designers poached by other businesses if your pipeline of upcoming projects isn't exciting enough for them. If work has become repetitive, they will seek out new experiences. Regardless of the situation, you need to be ready to react before your projects get derailed. You can do this by looking ahead and pre-empting and preparing for such eventualities.

The Solution

During the hiring process, you must evaluate the potential of candidates by assessing their values, behaviours, knowledge and skills. Essentially, you're trying to predict the future performance of a candidate based on their past performance when reading through their CV and viewing their portfolio of previous work.

Reviewing potential candidates and then carrying out the process of interviewing are very time-consuming activities on top of your already busy schedule. So, depending on the level of the role, you may not need to be directly involved in the initial review of candidates (unless they will be your direct reports), but it's important for you to agree on checkpoints in the process. This enables you to monitor for quality of decision-making, in the selection of candidates for interview, for example, so that you can check all is in order, even if you don't attend the first round. However, you should certainly be involved in the second or final round of interviews.

Requesting to see samples of design work before the interview process can help to significantly reduce the time involved in recruiting as you can quickly assess if they reach the necessary level of design skills. When recruiting for more senior roles in design management, it is still desirable to see samples of past projects because it can be beneficial for a design leader to be technically skilled. This helps them to build respect within the team and enables them to properly mentor designers in the finer technical aspects of design.

The interview then gives you the opportunity to evaluate the candidate in the moment and assess how they perform under pressure; an indicator of future performance. Values and knowledge lie within the candidate, and you need to understand how these aspects could play out through their behaviour and skills. Behaviours are arguably enablers for skills development, so poor behaviour could restrict the individual's potential for learning. And, unfortunately, behaviours are extremely difficult to alter, whereas skills can be acquired and improved. This is why assessing their attitude is so critical. The consequences of a poor attitude could be far-reaching and detrimental to the team and the organisation.

It is also worth considering the following points when you're searching for the best candidate:

Always keep an eye out for potential hires

You need to be constantly looking for new talent, whether it's in-house or in other companies. Then you'll be ready to approach the right people whenever the need arises rather than relying on them coming to you. Otherwise, when you have a gap in your team, it could take you months to gain momentum and hire the right person.

Success attracts talent

Try to build a strong team reputation from a track record of delivering well-received, commercially successful products which delight consumers and win design awards. Success helps to attract talent.

Understand the need

Carry out a SWOT analysis of your team's strengths, weaknesses, opportunities and threats so that you are clear about the current situation, including what they lack and what they need. This will help you to focus clearly on the type of candidate you are searching for to make the team whole. What is their unique talent which they'll bring to the team? What is their differentiating quality or skill that makes them shine? Will this complement your team or duplicate an already existing team strength?

How will they fit within the team and company?

Consider how a new recruit will fit into the existing unit and company. They won't join in a vacuum. They are part of a team and an organisational context. How will the new role impact the dynamics? How will interactions change and adapt? Do they fit with the company culture? Do they have a great work ethic that aligns with your current team's attitude? When you screen CVs and portfolios for potential new recruits, be clear about what you want your candidates to provide. Consider the different scenarios and outcomes of bringing in a senior versus a more junior individual. The more senior recruit may bring in more experience and knowledge, for example, but they could destabilise the others if they feel under threat, meaning the whole team becomes less productive.

Finding potential rather than established talent

Some of your best future employees won't necessarily be working at leading brands. They might be diamonds in the rough, waiting to be spotted and nurtured in order to achieve their full potential. So, don't always fixate on hiring recruits which already have the big agency and brand names on their CVs. They will demand the highest salaries and may require more incentives to join. There is more talent out there than you might imagine. Finding them is a nuanced skill, but it has huge rewards.

Setting a project for the interview is a great way to test someone's natural ability. Established people can hide behind a portfolio and claim they've done more work than they actually have, whereas those who haven't yet built up their portfolio could shine in this environment.

Beware of selfishness

Be wary of a candidate who doesn't give credit to fellow workers or give examples of working with others to achieve results. The ideal candidate

DESIGN LEAD SUCCEED

needs to be able to collaborate and see themselves as one part of a whole. A person who operates like a maverick could create silos in project work by withholding information and not sharing problems until it's too late.

Search for initiative
Look for examples of initiative in the candidate. They should be able to get on and complete a job without too much supervision, even if they are at a junior level. All new recruits need time to transition and embed themselves within the team, but then they need to begin performing, being proactive and looking for opportunities with the minimum of supervision. The alternative could have a huge impact, draining you of your time and energy as team lead, rather than freeing you up to drive the strategy forward.

Do they align with the mission and shared principles?
When you finally hire the best candidate, there will be a greater chance of them staying longer if their personal values align with the mission and shared principles of the business and team. So, even at interview stage, share these and gauge their connection to them.

Consider more flexible arrangements
Sometimes a new recruit is not the answer. There can be greater flexibility and efficiency in bringing freelancers or contractors on board on a temporary basis, as you can then upsize or downsize your team based on need. This also opens up the possibility of working with a designer who may be too expensive to hire full-time. But beware of the downsides. There are criteria that you must meet in the UK to obey tax rules, and you should only consider this if they fit within the dynamics and culture of your team. Otherwise, they can become destructive influences. And remember, too, that by relying on in-house talent, you will be retaining the knowledge and skills that they've built with you for the long term.

Preparing for interview
You should prepare well for the interview, setting questions which probe areas of behaviour, knowledge, skills and values, because this is your one chance to gauge their suitability. A well-planned set of questions allows the interview to flow, saves time and also enables you to spend more of your mental energy getting to know the candidate and drawing out indicators of their behaviour. It's useful to use the same questions with each candidate so that a direct comparison can be made. Interview with a colleague rather than on your own, as you'll be able to compare judgements and bat around ideas that could support the final decision.

Drawing It All Together

It's critical to assemble the correct mix of high-performing people within your team. This is because the strength of your creative output is directly correlated to these individuals and how they mesh together in their daily working practices. Be vigilant for change, which can disrupt your team's balance at any moment, and be prepared to react swiftly. Finally, never underestimate the importance of professional and positive behaviours in potential recruits, as they will determine how well they fit within your organisation. Skills can be taught; behaviour is harder to change. So, maximise every opportunity you have within the recruitment process to gauge new recruits' attitudes; they are a great indicator of their future performance.

12 KNOW YOUR TEAM'S PERSONALITIES

'When a team is made up of individuals with diverse personalities, backgrounds, and skills, they bring a rich tapestry of ideas and approaches that can lead to breakthrough innovations.'

FRANS JOHANSSON

What Is the Rule?

Getting to grips with your team's individual personality traits (as well as your own) and how they impact their behaviour as a group will enable you to get the best out of them as a manager and guide them through clashes and crises. Moreover, providing your team with a greater understanding of themselves and others will improve their communication and collaboration. It will also help them to consider the complexities of the user experience in any project, thus improving their design skills.

The Problem

Diverse personalities aren't a bad thing. The continuous tension between differing points of view arguably leads to better design solutions and greater levels of creativity. But when we interact with people who are very different to us, we often experience complexity and frustration. So, the more we understand ourselves and others, and are thus able to negotiate the conflicts this presents, the better our outcomes are going to be. The increasingly diverse methods of communication we now use, often virtually, also need to be considered because these can help but also hinder progress. Personality clashes between individuals within the team, and with external function team members, can be a continuous drain of management time. Trust can quickly erode in these situations, leading to breakdowns in project progress.

The Solution

Possessing a clearer understanding of your team's individual personalities and how they differ from yours will be invaluable in helping you to lead day to day. You'll have a greater appreciation of what communication style, approach or technique will be the most effective in any particular situation. For example, you may allow introverts the space and time to consider solutions before regrouping as a team.

As the design leader, it is essential that you have a good understanding of your own personality traits too. This is key because it is the filter through which you see the world and judge the actions of others. There are various methodologies available for assessing personality, such as Myers-Briggs and the Big Five Aspects Scale personality survey. Each comes with its own benefits and associated costs. There are many more, but select the methodology which best suits your situation and budget.

Then consider implementing the tests as follows:

Understanding the individual – Administer the personality test to each member of the team so that they may discover where they lay along the scale. Allow them sufficient time to digest and reflect on the information before sharing it with the wider group for further analysis whilst giving consideration to the necessary level of personal confidentiality. It's important that they complete the test truthfully so the results are worthwhile.

Understanding the team – With individual personality tests complete, it's then a good time to organise a team workshop to explore both the meaning behind the different personality traits and how their personalities compare and interact with the personality traits of others. It is beneficial to use an external facilitator for this exercise because they can bring greater and more in-depth expertise, offer a neutral voice to the team and allow you to step back and observe the results. The outputs of this analysis can address any major behavioural issues and personality clashes within the team which are currently damaging progress.

Using a formal personality test helps you to create a framework and common language from which to discuss ongoing adjustments to behaviour and personal development within the team. After this, further tests using different methodologies can be useful as they serve to provide confirmation of traits you have already identified.

Working practice – Once you have the results of their individual personality traits and the dynamics created by this, you can take this into account when you decide how best to tailor the work and the environment to get the best from this particular team. The set-up of the design studio environment should have variety and allow for different personalities and working preferences. This greater understanding of personality traits and psychology will also help the team to work in different areas of the design creation process, such as user testing and interviews, where these topics are central. They should have a better grasp of their target consumers and hence they should be able to create more appropriate and fulfilling user experiences.

Drawing It All Together

Discovering your personality make-up and that of your team will help to unblock friction between people and accelerate personal and team productivity on design projects. But in order to make these personal discoveries, you must commit, as design leader, to making it an ongoing, long-term journey of discovery and not merely a one-day event which is quickly forgotten. The process will not only make individual designers more aware of their personal behaviours and traits, but it will go some way towards advancing their understanding of how the very people they design for function.

The fact that everyone is different should be celebrated because of the diverse ways of thinking and design approaches that this brings. You should encourage everyone in the team to see this difference for the opportunity it is, rather than a drawback, and exercise an open mind without judgement.

13 SET OUT YOUR TEAM STRUCTURE

'For ordinary people to do extraordinary things, a system –
"a way of doing things" – is absolutely essential.'

MICHAEL E. GERBER

What Is the Rule?

A clearly defined team structure brings order, control and efficiency to the design creation process by confirming team reporting lines which connect each individual's role and responsibilities.

The Problem

The success of your leadership hinges on your ability to effectively communicate with and mobilise your team towards your business objectives. But, as the design team grows in terms of the number of team members and the different design disciplines covered, it will become impossible for you to individually manage each individual because of your limited time. This is where team structure comes in, setting out responsibilities, lines of communication and chains of command. A large design team without a defined team structure is unorganised chaos.

The Solution

Organisational structure is a good thing because it holds the interrelating elements, or in this case the people, firmly together. The often-chaotic practice of design creation should definitely be underpinned by the solid foundations of a clear team structure to help ensure efficient and effective information flow within the design team and between them and others.

Structure helps to mobilise a team, speeding up communication and minimising miscommunication.

The concept of team structure originally comes from the military, where it has been extensively trialled and tested and where highly complex objectives are achieved in the most difficult and pressurised of situations. It should include:

- Team and organisational hierarchy with defined job titles.
- Management reporting lines within the structure.

Here are some considerations when creating an effective design team structure:

From generalists to specialists – When a design team is small in terms of the number of designers, and there are multiple design disciplines and types of product categories to be covered, it's necessary for the designers to operate as 'generalists'. This means they can be flexible and multiskilled across different areas of design. But as a design team grows, there may be an opportunity to structure the team in a way which designates 'specialists' to different design disciplines and types of product categories such as footwear, apparel and equipment etc. This is an important consideration when defining your team structure because designers working as specialists have the potential to deliver better results. Their likely passion for and daily, repetitive practice in that subject means these individuals are more knowledgeable and skilled in that area. Although, with this benefit comes the drawback that their contribution can be more difficult to replace if they leave the team.

Succession planning – To aid the future stability of your team and to reduce the need to always seek costly and time-consuming external recruitment, your team structure should build in routes for succession as individuals move out or upwards. This approach of succession planning can help to retain skills and knowledge within the team – very valuable when operating a structure with specialist designers as mentioned previously. A succession plan is essential, even for your own role, because it provides a second in command for periods of holidays or illness, for example. It is easier to build a succession plan for senior roles when you have a larger design team because there will be multiple layers of reporting lines within the different design disciplines. So, when an individual moves out or up, there is already an identified individual who is ready to succeed to the vacant position.

Hire leaders who you can trust – When your team is large enough to require heads of various design disciplines, you need to carefully consider the best person for the job. You will be entirely reliant on these direct reports to communicate your message to their teams without adding too much of their own spin, so it's important they are aligned with your vision and can be relied on. You need to trust these individuals implicitly. From experience, I would only have a maximum of six direct reports as a leader so you have the time to collaborate closely. Four maximum is ideal.

Choose a structure – There are various types of structures to choose from. Without a formal hierarchy, the approach could be termed a 'flat structure', which is common in smaller teams. This is perfectly valid and it aids collaboration in many circumstances because all the individuals occupy the same level of seniority, reducing the need for additional communication through multiple levels. However, it tends to undermine personal development, learning and growth because individuals have less opportunity to lead projects or people. This is something that could really benefit an organisation and which many people seek. A functional structure, on the other hand, groups common design specialities together in sub-teams. In a design organisation, this might be industrial design, graphic design, apparel design, footwear design and design engineering, for example. This hierarchy allows for promotion and progression within sub-teams for designers before they then take on a wider remit for overall design.

Use formal hierarchy to manage team dynamics – People need to know where they sit within the hierarchy of the organisation. If there is a stable, reliable and trusted structure in place, it helps to manage egos within the team, leading to smoother collaboration and less infighting. In his book, *The Chimp Paradox*, Dr Steve Peters introduces the concept of the brain having different parts. Two influential parts are defined as the 'human' (frontal cortex) and the 'chimp' (limbic system). He describes the human part as working with logic and seeking fulfilment, whereas the chimp part works with emotion and seeks aspects such as survival. But, crucially, the chimp part is the strongest and often takes over control of our functioning if its basic needs are not met. If each role has undefined parameters, there is the potential for territory wars and land grabs. Structure also helps with setting and explaining wage levels so people can see there is a transparent and consistent ladder they are climbing. All of these benefits help to manage an individual's inner chimp.

Align with the organisation – Your team structure doesn't stand alone. It has to align and link up with the structure of the other functional teams within your organisation. Does it serve the needs of your team well in this respect, or does it create confusion and duplication of effort? The design structure should not be created in isolation for this reason; cross-functional working requires seamless communication and integration. So, to aid in smooth alignment with the wider organisation, it is vital that you share your structure and reporting lines with your counterparts from other functions. They can then inform their teams so lines of communication can be set up between the appropriate individuals. This aids productivity and prevents them from taking up your team's time unnecessarily.

Does the structure align with roles and responsibilities? – There can be a disconnect between what someone is tasked with doing and their standing in the hierarchy. If they are managing a project without the requisite power and level of authority, it might reduce their capacity to fulfil their responsibilities. If they are in a high-level position of power, they shouldn't be spending their time on smaller tasks and neglecting the direction and development of their reports.

Understand the power of job titles – A job title can have a significant impact on how an individual perceives themselves and their value to the company. For instance, if the 'senior' designation is removed from their title during a restructuring, it can create the impression of a demotion. The alignment of job titles with an individual's experience and skill level plays a significant role in influencing employee satisfaction.

Use the structure to motivate – When placing individuals into the structure, think about how best to motivate them to reach their potential and stay with the team and company. Consider the individual's circumstances, future career goals, potential next role and the time they've already invested in their current position. For example, if they want to manage a sub-team, consider allowing them to mentor the newest recruit in order to give them the experience they need.

Collaborate on the structure and get buy-in – Seek upward and downward input when you're putting together the structure. Listen to all areas as everyone will be affected. Seek approval from the CEO and the HR team (as there may also be budget implications), and get buy-in from your direct design reports in the design management team as well as your cross-functional peers. Then share the proposed structure individually with team members before a formal announcement so that there are no shocks.

Embed the structure and make it visible – Once you have the structure, don't let it waste away on a shelf. Make sure it's at the forefront of people's minds by making diagrams easily visible and referring to them regularly. Diagrams are also necessary as when organisations grow and become larger, they are much more complex to manage. Visuals will give people a quick reference guide to the structure of other functions to aid the correct path of communication. For example, it might answer questions such as how external information like design briefs flow into the design team.

Drawing It All Together

It's essential to develop a robust and clear team structure as it becomes the pathway through which your leadership communication flows.

The aim of defining a team structure is to clarify lines of communication (internal and external), motivate and reassure your team and provide personal development.

However, remember that the 'perfect' structure doesn't exist. It's something that is individual to your team and which will need to be adjusted frequently when people leave and when the business grows or changes direction.

14 DEFINE ROLES AND RESPONSIBILITIES

'The strength of the wolf is the pack . . . On a football team, it's not the strength of the individual players but . . . the strength of the unit and how they all function together.'

BILL BELICHICK

What Is the Rule?

Roles and responsibilities define an individual's purpose within an organisation. This helps to remove ambiguity. This activity should be completed in combination with the creation of the team structure, which provides the framework within which the individual's role and specific details of their responsibilities are contained. When you have all the right people in the right roles, with clarity on where they are expected to operate, your design creation process will have a solid foundation.

The Problem

What would happen if none of the individuals in your team had a defined role? How would design projects progress? Chaos can often fuel creativity by randomly connecting diverse thoughts and ideas into new forms and meanings, but this same chaos can also stifle the effectiveness of a design team and their efficient execution of a brief.

If we were brainstorming creative ideas in our own minds or in an educational setting, with no parameters and the desire to experiment, a little bit of chaos would be a good thing. Within a commercial setting, however, there will be objectives for projects with defined deadlines and resources. The larger the organisation, the greater the number of projects and the greater the number of participating team members. This level of complexity can benefit from a higher level of organisation. Organisational team structures, which we explored in the last chapter, help to formalise each individual's position to a certain extent, but this does not specifically define their role and responsibilities on projects and how these responsibilities overlap and interconnect with the roles of others. Without these formalised rules and expectations, productivity can drop due to duplication, missed work or miscommunication, for example.

Relationships between team members can become strained if there are misunderstandings around each other's area of responsibility. From past experience, I believe over half of the interpersonal conflicts that arose within design teams and between design teams and other functions were due in part to this misalignment and skewed perceptions of each other's roles and areas of responsibility. This is possibly due to the fact that your role and area of responsibility becomes your 'territory', to protect and mark out, and this triggers a primal instinct in us as humans.

The Solution

Firstly, be clear about your own role and responsibilities as leader. This clarity then enables your design team's roles and responsibilities to dovetail into yours accordingly. As the 'chief design officer' or 'head of design', your role is to provide the creative vision for the design team but also for the entire organisation. In clearly defining the team's roles and responsibilities, your objective should be to create a state of order.

Consider the following when defining the roles and responsibilities of your team:

Communicate with them in writing – Make roles and responsibilities more explicit by documenting them clearly and making them readily available to everyone. Verbal acknowledgement of responsibilities is not enough!

Make sure there is alignment – Make sure that the responsibilities you give to one person align and integrate with the other individuals within your design team. But also consider the impact on other functions within the organisation. Conflicts may arise if different functions believe that they own specific activities and tasks. It's important that, as a leader, you connect with other functional leaders to ensure alignment from the top downwards.

Leave room for flexibility – Be open to adjusting the responsibilities that are defined for each person – have an agile and not a fixed mentality. Roles will evolve and change over time, and flexibility leaves room for creativity and innovation. It's important to regularly review and adjust them in order to reflect how things are.

Utilise performance reviews – Annual performance objectives can be set against areas of responsibility, which will help to underline and embed each person's role.

Reiterate roles to keep order – People need clear realms of ownership. Without this, 'territory' is left up for grabs, and conflicts may occur when people try to 'protect' what they feel is theirs. As I previously mentioned, these primal instincts are strong, and this is where formal 'roles' can maintain equilibrium. It is important to regularly reiterate the roles and responsibilities to the team to maintain order. For example, this can be done whenever an individual accrues new responsibilities in a promotion or if someone leaving the team changes the roles of those left behind.

Give them ownership – It is important to discuss the roles and responsibilities with the individuals involved and engage with them in their creation so that they have a certain level of choice and input. Ownership and autonomy can be a strong motivation for an individual. It's also useful to allow them to develop their passions by including a chosen area of knowledge within their responsibilities. In the past, I've named people 'team experts'. In this way, you are keeping them fulfilled while benefitting the team with more specialist support.

Use it to frame their personal development – Clear roles and responsibilities can also be an opportunity to provide development and growth to team members. Over time, their responsibilities can be increased, in a visible and formal way, to reflect their increased skills and competency.

Drawing It All Together

Clearly understood roles and responsibilities provide individuals with clarity around their own purpose and mission. This contributes to a smoother design creation process overall. The documentation of design roles and responsibilities also serves as a reference point for discussion if disputes over ownership of workload arise; it also saves you time as the design leader in having to write job descriptions from scratch when recruitment is necessary. But one of the greatest advantages for you as a leader is that there's potentially less need for intrusive management check-ins because designers are clearer on their direction and can operate with relative autonomy.

15 HELP YOUR TEAM TO REACH THEIR MAXIMUM POTENTIAL

'Your talent determines what you can do. Your motivation determines how much you are willing to do. Your attitude determines how well you do it.'

LOU HOLTZ

What Is the Rule?

If you can harness the creative potential of every designer in your team and focus their minds on the team's objectives, you will ultimately meet and surpass the organisation's objectives. In creating tailored and robust personal objectives, you will help individuals to grow and they will feel valued in contributing to the company's success.

The Problem

An unfocussed and undirected team whose personal objectives aren't aligned with the overall mission of the organisation will not deliver exceptional outputs. Creative individuals naturally love to explore and experiment, but their energies and creations can unintentionally follow their own meandering preferences and motives if left unchecked. If individuals aren't coordinated in their efforts towards a common goal, your organisation will struggle to meet its objectives.

The Solution

Coordinating every individual within an organisation, with the goal of maximising their contributions towards the mission and objectives of the organisation, is termed as 'performance management'. This approach is critical in large organisations, which are often unwieldy and require a common focus to keep everyone on track, but it can also be very beneficial in smaller organisations and design teams.

In the main, this approach is welcomed by the designers that I have worked with because it helps them to define their individual purpose within the organisation. They can see the direct line between their contributions and the organisation's overall objectives – a tangible example of how they are supporting the delivery of results. Often, when there was a delay in setting out my team's personal objectives for the year, there were murmurings of anxiety and frustration. They felt dissatisfied with not having clear visibility in terms of what they were aiming for and where to focus their attention. Once the personal objectives had been set, they became noticeably more relaxed, happier and motivated. They were keen to progress in achieving them as they knew they would provide personal growth and development along the way.

Consider the following when creating personal objectives for your team:

Start from the top – Ascertain the organisation's mission and strategic objectives, then use these to define the design function objectives. Then the individual design team members' objectives can be defined. Build these objectives with the designers – ultimately asking them to write them – so that they have input into how to mould the approach. This will increase their buy-in and motivation.

Use a simple tracking mechanism – Use a standardised document which is visual, short and simple to complete. Objectives might be focused on design projects, design process and tools and also areas of specialism and areas for personal development.

Share objectives – Make sure there is visibility of each individual's objectives for the wider design team so it's easy to check alignment and ensure there are no duplications of workload. Be sensitive to the feelings of individuals and do not share development objectives which are aimed at working on improving specific skills or behaviours.

Push them to reach their potential – Ensure they are 'stretch' objectives with clear definitions of what successfully reaching the objective will look like. This means they should not be easy to attain and that the individual has to push their capabilities to achieve them. These types of objectives are beneficial in two ways. Firstly, they are more motivating, and secondly, they increase the potential of the organisation.

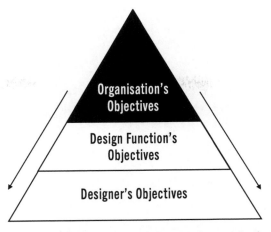

Figure 15.1 The alignment of designers' objectives to the organisation's objectives

Make their success measurable – It is important to set deadlines for their personal objectives that are in line with the set durations of the organisation's objectives. These tend to be annual targets and then medium to longer-term objectives. Ensure all individual objectives are easily measurable against time in this way as well as against other parameters such as cost, quality and behaviours.

Review them regularly – Take time out to meet with individuals to see how they're doing and whether they need to change or update their objectives. This is extremely important because it sends the message to the designer that you care about them and their objectives. Celebrate successes and define necessary improvements for individuals when they reach deadlines.

Drawing It All Together

If you help people to focus their attention on achieving the company's objectives, you'll have an engaged team who are more highly skilled individuals at the end of each project. It shows that you care and that you take an interest in them. They will tend to stay with the group for longer and contribute more of themselves. As a leader, you will also benefit from feeling more secure and confident that the important tasks are being attended to.

16 ESTABLISH A CULTURE OF LEARNING

'Man is constantly growing. And when he is bound by a set pattern of ideas or way of doing things, that's when he stops growing.'

BRUCE LEE

What Is the Rule?

It is vital to always encourage your team to keep bettering themselves by providing a learning environment which offers formal and informal training opportunities. Ramping up your design team's knowledge and skills will translate into better designed and more desirable product creations. Also, one of the fastest routes to personal improvement is through formal training; by nurturing and supporting team members in this way, they will be happier, more fulfilled and loyal to the company.

The Problem

Change is constant. Technological advances are relentless. They are driven not only by the 'technology push' of new innovations released into the marketplace, but also by the constant 'consumer pull' from the public who demand the latest products. And importantly, the methodologies and tools at a designer's disposal are ever improving and broadening. For example, the use of artificial intelligence (AI) powered software for generating design and artwork has become freely available, which opens up a new channel of opportunity for raising the level of design exploration and execution. If your design team are not continuing to learn and improve their skills, you are not only standing still but falling behind while the rest of your industry advances. You might still believe that you can generate novel ideas and join the dots because of your innate creativity as a team, but if you aren't aware of the dots available to you, then you will eventually become obsolete.

The Solution

It's important to integrate learning into your culture so that it becomes an ongoing and normalised behaviour for your team. Through team learning, prioritising constant growth ensures that you always stay at the forefront of your industry. But be aware that lack of time can be a huge problem when trying to include learning in your team's schedule. For example, formal training was rarely available when I worked in design consultancies because the team was busy and there was a constant pipeline of projects that needed to be quickly delivered to clients. We acquired design skills by observing and interacting with more senior colleagues and then putting them into practice on live projects. And then, when I couldn't learn through others because the particular skills I desired were not present within the business, I searched for formal training during my personal time. For example, at one point I didn't possess 3D CAD modelling skills because this wasn't part of my university course and, as it was the early days of this technology in the 1990s, there was less opportunity in the workplace to learn it. However, I knew this skill was critical for my future career, so I sacrificed my personal time and money to do a course.

Learning can be categorised into three components: behaviours, skills and knowledge.

Consider the following when implementing design team learning in these three components, whether formal or informal:

Formal training

● **Utilise online classes** – Training doesn't always have to be classroom-based and in-person if time is the enemy and you don't have the resources to invest. There are online courses available from multiple sources that are much more flexible and which cover the whole gamut of subjects, whether it's design skills in crafts, software, theory or design management. Almost all design industry organisations also seem to offer courses aiming to upskill designers and design leaders.

● **Apply training to live projects** – It can be useful to apply training modules to the projects you are currently working on so that up-to-date knowledge can benefit the project as well as helping the team member to learn. I personally invested in a part-time distance learning MBA. The modules allowed me to study and apply theory to live projects, which benefitted both my grades and my employer at the time.

● **Assess project weaknesses to choose training** – This is a really practical way of choosing when to add training and what it should be. If the required knowledge and skills are not in the team, you have a need that must be filled and you can invest in a course knowing it will pay off in the long-run.

Informal training

• **Learn from others** – This is probably the most effective method of informal training as it utilises the resources you already have. Set up coaching and mentoring from colleagues in the design team or from others in the organisation.

• **Learn from practice** – We might talk about training as a separate activity, but our day-to-day work is probably our main method of gaining new knowledge. On-the-job designing, when we are constantly being challenged by new projects, will instil vital lessons and push us to learn new approaches and skills.

• **Utilise training twice** – Ask any individuals who receive formal training to share the learning and course notes with the rest of the team for reference. In this way, knowledge can 'cascade' through the group, saving time and resources.

• **Learn through new recruits** – Bringing expertise into the team via new recruits is another method of acquiring new ways of working which can be adopted by the wider team. They will have a different set of skills, experience and training that they can share.

• **Provide resources for learning** – Every design office should have a library that's brimming with reference material for inspiration.

Drawing It All Together

Building a culture of learning is a win-win for you and your team. Often, investment in training pays for itself within a short period of time. In bringing new ways of thinking, behaviour and skills into the team, you can reduce timelines, save costs and improve design creation quality. It also helps to build loyalty from your team because you have invested in their development. Their wellbeing and happiness will increase, and the team's culture will blossom.

17 ADVISE TEAM MEMBERS SENSITIVELY

'Giving advice is like playing pinball: only by pushing and pulling can you encourage the ball to go in a new direction and increase your score. But too much pushing and pulling can cause a tilt and stop the game.'

CHIP R. BELL

What Is the Rule?

Monitoring and coordinating your team is critical to your leadership responsibilities during the design creation process. From time to time, you may have to step in if an individual's work or behaviour is negatively impacting a project or the relationships within the team. If you're able to give them advice in the right way, at the right time, you should be able to help them grow and also maintain team morale and progress. However, it's also full of risk as you could easily damage their confidence and trust in you. Managing team interactions is a hugely complex task for a leader as we are all complicated and diverse human beings.

The Problem

It may be necessary for individuals to make adjustments to their way of working or their behaviour for the future success of design projects and for their own personal development. For example, junior designers can sometimes become too emotionally invested in their own concepts during the ideation phase of projects. If their ideas aren't selected and taken forward, they may find it difficult to accept. In this situation, they may need to be reminded of the project brief and the need for the best solution to be selected for the benefit of the business. They must understand that even though there is still a level of subjectivity in the final selection, it is the responsibility of the relevant design manager or creative director to make that choice, and this should be respected. As another example, you may have designers who suffer from poor time management and an inability to prioritise, resulting in missed deadlines and lower quality work. It's your job as leader to bring this up with them in order to resolve the issue. However, this is wrought with problems and can easily damage their confidence and self-belief if they take a hit to their ego. If you lose their trust and they become demotivated, you are compounding the problem. But if you avoid resolving the issue, it could grow into something much more destructive, which could lead to project failure or the loss of key talent.

The Solution

Ultimately, giving advice to an individual may be what is right and best for them as a person. It is also likely critical for the success of the team, which needs to be kept in balance and harmony in order to perform to its highest potential. But be acutely aware that the timing at which advice is given to an individual can make a significant difference to how well the advice is received and thus their future performance.

Any corrective advice should be given because it provides a long-term benefit to the individual that underlines how much you care about their personal development. For example, this might be highlighting their areas of unconscious incompetence (what they don't know they don't know), such as a lack of project management skills or speaking down to colleagues by using a 'parental' tone of voice which damages relationships. Alternatively, it could be calling out their conscious and deliberate behaviours which negatively impact the dynamics and performance of the wider team. This might be their tendency to undermine colleagues in meetings or to purposely ignore instructions for design changes in favour of their own personal agenda.

Consider these suggestions when preparing to provide advice to one of your team:

Ascertain different views of the situation – When receiving news of an issue from another individual, try to understand the situation and their possible motives for sharing. This is only one opinion, so you should make efforts to find out the opinions of others for a more balanced view.

Pick your battles – Sometimes you need to pick your battles because too much interference in team dynamics will make you seem like a micro-manager, damaging your working relationship with the individual and knocking their confidence and motivation to be proactive. If the likelihood and impact of the risk is minimal, no advice or action might be the best option.

Do you need to monitor the situation? – Early intervention is ideal, but sometimes events need to play out a little longer for the risk to escalate into an issue so that you have something concrete to work with. This is because a behavioural issue may be a one-off or minor, but if repeated often it becomes a bigger problem. Remember, these are only the risks or issues that you've been made aware of. Depending on how large your team is and the communication tools in place, it might be that there are other issues that will surface if you keep an eye on the situation. If witnessing an event firsthand, you may wish to wait and see if the event happens again or enquire with another witness to see if it's happened before.

Consider timing – The timing of how advice is given should take variables into consideration such as the likelihood and impact of the risk if you do not intervene, their personality, experience and skill level and your relationship to and authority over the person involved.

Communicate the issue with care – The Centre for Creative Leadership's Situation-Behavior-Impact model (SBI)™ suggests a simple feedback process which I think works well. State the situation that is occurring and describe the impact that their behaviour is having on the project and wider organisation, utilising multiple sources of feedback. This ensures they understand it's not just your subjective opinion but rather it's based on the feelings of the wider team, which will hold more weight. It is also essential to provide the advice in private so that they do not feel self-conscious in the proximity of colleagues.

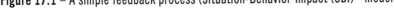

Figure 17.1 – A simple feedback process (Situation-Behavior-Impact (SBI)™ model)

Ask a specialist to mentor them – The advice you give them initially could be supported by coaching or mentoring from another technical expert in the team if the problem is design skills. This will reassure them it's not just an act of criticism but that you want to help them grow and learn.

Drawing It All Together

Giving feedback and advice to your team members when they need to improve is difficult, but it's often essential to get projects and relationships back on track. If you do it effectively, you can minimise delays and reduce the amount of wasted money from unnecessary mistakes. You'll also benefit from strengthened interpersonal relationships within the team.

SECTION

HOW TO BE A GREAT DESIGN LEADER

Having a great design team is not enough to achieve the best creative results. If your creative direction and design management abilities are lacking, then the team will never deliver to their true potential. As the design leader, it's your responsibility to establish an operational system which successfully directs and monitors the journey of the creative process through to completion. More than this, you need to be able to do it repeatedly, while ever evolving and improving.

The rules in this section of the book will help you to nurture those core design leadership skills.

DESIGN LEAD SUCCEED

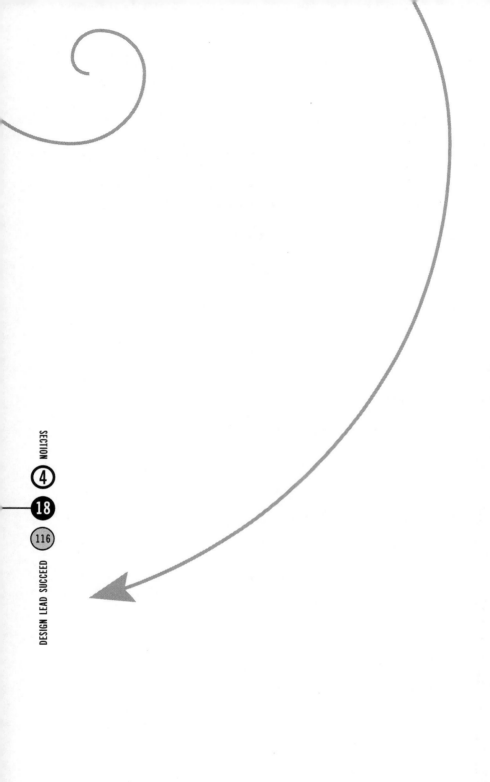

18 FIND BALANCE AND PROTECT YOUR RESILIENCE

'We must keep things in perspective. Balance is keeping things in perspective. Don't get carried away if things are going too well or too poorly. Don't get carried away, just continue or make the effort to do the best you can at whatever you're doing.'

JOHN WOODEN

What Is the Rule?

To lead well and consistently perform at your very best, you need to find and maintain your optimal work-life balance. Defining this balance provides the guard rails to help protect your mental and physical wellbeing and to keep you in the design game for the long-term. Resilience is critical to your success.

The Problem

For many of us, being a designer able to create every day is our driving passion. When we enjoy our work so much, it becomes a vocation and a calling, but it can easily become an obsession. Even as a designer, my role could become all-encompassing as there were never-ending details and solutions to projects to consider. As the design leader, you must consider these as well as the team in your care. You have ultimate responsibility for the performance of the design function as a whole and obligations to the wider business. If you own the business, then you will have additional pressures that will drive you to sacrifice your personal time in the short to medium-term because of the potential future rewards.

Whether the pace and intensity of your work is sustainable is of course based on your own judgement and how you feel. Every organisation and project are different in the way they will test you. For example, if you are working in fashion design, driven by collections for the seasons of spring/summer and autumn/winter, the intensity of your work may be cyclical. Or the intensity could depend on the specific project. For example, it might be high-risk, urgent or on a large scale, such as products for a global event like the Olympic games where the deadline cannot be moved. Everyone is unique, with varying tolerances to mental and physical stress, but occasionally our workload may become overwhelming and unmanageable. More often than not, these flashes of emotion ran through me at times when I had been promoted to a new role or began work at a new organisation. They threw me into a steep learning curve until I became more familiar and proficient with the task at hand. But what helped me to remain relatively calm in these situations was to remember that I could only try my best. You can only do what you can do. When you reach this point, and there is still a shortfall in terms of work that needs to be completed or the performance level that's required, then it is time to step back, reassess the situation and perhaps explore alternative solutions to delivering your workload with the assistance of colleagues or a mentor.

The Solution

It is important to gauge your threshold for physical and emotional stress. I have found this has become easier with age and greater experience. Knowing when to say 'no' is critical. And it's important to realise that saying 'no' is not a sign of weakness but of strength. An inexperienced designer may feel afraid to say 'no' because they think it makes them look like a failure or incapable. They may not have the tools to articulate the very valid reasons why they are saturated with workload. It helps to follow up the 'no' with logical and factual information that demonstrates your needs against the parameters of time, cost and quality. It is far better to raise your hand early and admit that you need support than to carry on and underdeliver at too late a stage, which could jeopardise the state of the whole project. As the leader, you need to recognise this issue before it arises in others as well as in yourself.

Figure 18.1 provides a reminder of our priorities in life which can help us to maintain balance. Your health should always be your primary concern. Without good mental and physical health, the rest of our lives become more difficult or impossible. From personal experience, after a process of reflecting on my values, I realised that health and fitness should be a core priority. I then realised that I was investing proportionally far more time and money into other areas of my life such as hobbies. While this fulfilled my values of creativity and discovery, it meant I was neglecting my health, so I redressed the balance. Then there is the next priority of

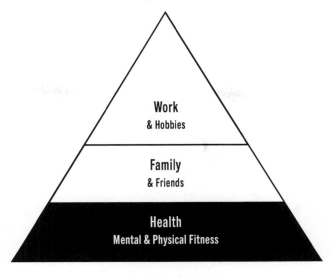

Figure 18.1 Life priorities chart

your family, close friends and relationships. These people (and pets) are hugely important to your happiness, and you must ensure that you invest time in maintaining these connections. Then there is your work and hobbies. You might have a number of different ones of varying priority in your life. You might also be fortunate enough to have a job which is also your hobby. I have been lucky enough to experience this in my career when I worked as a designer for Speedo. Swimming became my life seven days a week. Everyone is different and has a bespoke situation, but it is important to periodically review how much of your time and financial investment is going into the different key areas of your life.

Here are a few suggestions for finding balance and protecting your resilience:

Keep in mind your personal values and targets in your design role

You don't want to become rudderless. You need to take responsibility for your own career. What do you aim to accomplish? Set yourself a timescale for what you want to achieve while in the role. Set guard rails for the job. What are your expectations? What are you not prepared to compromise on? At what point will these reflections instigate your search for a new role elsewhere? You have your own personal values, and so does the organisation that you work for. Ideally, you will already share many of the values of the organisation, which is why it is a good fit for you. But be conscious of and check if the organisation changes course and loses sight of its (and therefore your) values. If this is not something you can help influence and correct, then knowing when you are ready to leave is a good mark in the sand to have. Otherwise, you might drift for far too long and realise that you have lost precious time invested in the wrong venture.

Always work on yourself in addition to your job

Your own personal growth is just as important as your growth in the job. Getting the balance right is important. For example, I studied for and personally funded an MBA. It was not conventional for a designer to want to study a master's in business management. I felt that I needed to gain a broader understanding of business and how design fit into that formula, and that was enough to set aside time and resources.

Separate your work life from your personal life

You need to be able to separate yourself from the business for periods of time in order to switch off from work and maintain a balanced perspective on life. Work is not the only thing in your life, and it will dampen your creativity if you don't experience anything outside of it. Goals outside of your job will help you to prioritise time away from work. For example, signing up to a challenge that inspires you can be a great distraction and can improve your personal resilience. I swam in a relay team across the Channel from England to France for charity some years ago. Looking back on this experience, I have come to realise how pivotal it was in maintaining my mental health and recovery during what was a particularly stressful period in my life. The physical and psychological challenge of training in the cold waters helped to focus my thoughts and gave me mental respite from personal and financial issues. Being around a new group of people in the challenge also helped a great deal.

Establish a daily routine

Spend some time establishing a daily routine which works for you as an individual. Personally, I know I get the best out of myself and the day with an early rise and a gym session before heading into the office if I'm not working from home. I will aim to think through my most difficult planning tasks in the morning when I am mentally fresh.

Get enough sleep and eat well

Sleep and a good diet are crucial to your wellbeing and happiness. If you are not looking after yourself, you will see an imbalance in your life and your resilience will be undermined. It's often useful to monitor and track your sleep so you're aware if there's a problem brewing. It's also good to set aside time to feed yourself healthy food – fuel to keep your mind and body running efficiently. It's important to recognise signs of imbalance in the lives of your team too. Be empathetic and realistic with the workload you impose on them.

Track your progress in a combined list of goals

Add your personal goals to your work goals if you use lists. This will help them to remain at the forefront of your mind each day to help maintain perspective.

Drawing It All Together

By using the suggestions given and putting up guard rails to help you navigate life, it should help you to regularly take a step back and see the context of your situation clearly. This will enable you to remain resilient and to regularly confirm if the leadership role you have is still right for you or if the situation has changed. You may decide to move on because you have accomplished what you originally set out to do, and that's fine. Maintaining balance will mean you don't lose perspective.

To stay on top of your game, your routine or approach needs to be sustainable in the long-run.

19 WIDEN YOUR NETWORK AND DEVELOP ALLIES

'Slow down and make building relationships as important as building projects.'

GREG MORTENSON

What Is the Rule?

Grow a network of contacts in and around your organisation. A percentage of these contacts will develop into strong alliances that will help you to navigate business and design challenges which come your way. This will aid your growth as a design leader and enhance the quality of the creative output from your team.

The Problem

We don't have all the answers. Our business lives and careers are wrought with challenges. Whether recognised or hidden, these challenges can present barriers to the successful creation and launch of any new product. Although all problems can eventually be overcome with skill and experience, they can often be resolved with greater speed, less cost and better results if we have stronger relationships to draw on. We are social and political animals at heart, and by embedding ourselves into the 'society' of our organisations and industry, we can thrive.

The Solution

Spending time building a wide network of contacts and strong alliances will allow you to navigate challenges and capitalise on opportunities that might pass others by. Your network connects you to sources of informal information which are not readily available to others, thereby benefiting you.

Whenever I am asked to be a visiting lecturer, I always remind students of the future potential power of the network of contacts they will make through their current course of study and with their peers. Social networking sites have made building and maintaining these contacts simpler than ever before, so it is much easier to benefit from your student network as your career progresses. Compare this to when I studied design at university in the mid-90s. It was the early days of the internet and social media wasn't even a thing. I look back now and realise that I had my own ready-made network on that design course. Each one of the 40 individuals on it had a good chance of graduating and securing a job in the creative industries. But I didn't make a great effort to keep in touch with everyone. It was more labour intensive to do so with phone calls. Even so, a couple of years after graduating, while in a design role, I was offered an opportunity to interview for a new role through a university connection. This demonstrates the power of networks in your career.

Internal connections can help us on a project and organisational level. It might be that it can enable you to negotiate timeline extensions, more budget allocation and greater team support because of the goodwill that you've nurtured. As a design leader, you might be able to generate greater influence for the design team. External connections can introduce you to wider networks with all sorts of possibilities. These might open up leads for finding new talent for your team or offer you client or career opportunities that are not advertised or publicly available. For example, I've found the majority of temporary freelancers for my teams through recommendations that have been kindly shared by my design industry contacts. This has saved me a lot of time and the additional costs of advertising.

As a leader, external connections also offer personal benefits. It can sometimes be a lonely place as a creative manager. Having a counterpart to share problems with from another organisation, or from another function of the business, can be of great help in letting off steam or providing you with a sounding board.

Consider the following aspects that will help you to network and build alliances more successfully:

• Attend internal training courses in your organisation where you can meet and get to know colleagues on a deeper level.
• Volunteer for additional responsibilities and events that bring you into contact with other colleagues around the business.
• Social media platforms, and in particular LinkedIn, are invaluable channels through which to build your personal profile as a design leader and to connect and grow your network.
• Contribute as a speaker to industry events where you will come into contact with peers from other organisations and industries.

- It is easier to grow your network within your organisation with colleagues on your level or below. It can be more difficult to grow your network upwards, so always remember that your boss or direct line manager must not be compromised. Whoever they are and however they operate, it is you who must accommodate them and work to fit around them and their style. Building a stakeholder management plan helps you to visualise all of the stakeholders connected to your design team. This process helps you to visualise and understand how best to engage with these stakeholders in order to leverage the greatest benefits to the design function.
- Set up your own design knowledge sharing events within your organisation with the aim of swapping information and building skills for the benefit of the whole company. This approach can work well if your organisation contains multiple business units or brands with separate design teams.
- Try to meet regularly with other functional team leaders to discuss issues. These chats can be invaluable to quickly resolve issues between individuals or teams, and they may even defuse tensions before they arise. Alignment at the top like this can allow for easier integration, collaboration and productivity between the wider teams.

It's also important to note that there are limits when it comes to receiving beneficial information from your network. It's important that you always act with integrity and exercise your better judgement to avoid breaches of confidentiality. There are severe legal implications for such behaviour. If your network gives you advance knowledge of a company's future actions, this could allow you or someone else to unfairly profit, which is wrong on many levels and should be strictly avoided. This is probably best known in the financial sector as insider trading, but it's also highly relevant to the design industry where new concepts and products are highly guarded before their launch.

Drawing It All Together

It obviously takes time to build rapport and trust with people, and the emails, meetings, catch-ups and lunches that are required are not a small investment by any means. However, networks allow for more options and possibilities in any given situation, and they can help you thrive, overcome challenges and capitalise on opportunities. Your previous path was lit with a torch, but now, with a large set of strong relationships around you, you have a floodlight! Parts that were hidden suddenly become visible.

20 DELEGATE AND EMPOWER

'Absence of delegation will not just slow down your career advancement in management but will inevitably stop it dead in its tracks.'

JAMES JENKS & JOHN KELLY

What Is the Rule?

Delegation of tasks is not only necessary as a leader, it also empowers your team. This does not mean that you lose authority. Quite the opposite. You will be more likely to build trust, respect and loyalty from your team if you give them the power to deliver results.

The Problem

Although there are some design disciplines, such as jewellery making, where creating products on your own is possible, it's certainly more difficult. In the main, product creation is most effective when you have a team around you. You can't make every decision on your own. As the design leader, it is your job to get the most out of the individuals in your team so that you are not doing everything yourself. By harnessing and supporting their diverse experience, talents and expertise in different areas of the design creation process, you will develop a high-performing team which is self-sufficient. Micro-management, or instructing designers on exactly how they should perform each task in the way you prefer, is not always the best solution. It can damage the confidence of individuals, and it wastes their own unique skills and perspective. You do not have the time to be involved in all of the details. You need to be able to step back and see the bigger picture.

The Solution

In order to delegate and empower effectively, consider the following aspects:

Start with a clear direction – In order to delegate effectively, you need to be really clear on what your vision and objectives are for the short and long-term and how this translates into a strategy. You will need to be laser focussed on what you are creating and for whom, where and when. With this information, you will be ideally positioned to brief your team. The vision and objectives provide them with the context and the 'why' for the activity.

Provide clear timelines – You will also need to provide overall timelines and key milestones for your objectives. This should include measurable milestones and check-in points for achieving them. The team can then unpack these and build in more necessary detail to chart their progress, or you can do this with them to support the planning process.

Specify standards – You should specify the required output standards for the task and then ask them to achieve them. This provides clear parameters for success so they are empowered to reach a goal.

Consider each team member's competency – Do not tell experienced team members how to do a task when you delegate. They will often surprise you and achieve it in a novel manner that you would never have expected. Part of delegation is trusting their expertise and potential to rise to a task. However, an exception to the rule is a new recruit or junior designer who may need to be given more specific instructions. They don't yet have the experience or the skillsets to be able to achieve the same results that you could, so leaving them without support is irresponsible. You will need to suggest and demonstrate a method for achieving the goal from which they can learn and grow.

Follow up – It's really important to agree on when you will check in with them and review their progress. This gives them reassurance that you will support and guide them if needed as well as taking an interest in their progress. This also helps you to relax a little as a leader because you know there is a formal process of control and monitoring in place.

Drawing It All Together

In delegating tasks, you will empower your team. The results of this are powerful. You can maintain a clear focus on the bigger picture without drowning in the details of every project, which is essential to successful leadership. Importantly, you will also have a highly-motivated, engaged and driven team who are happy in their work. The results of this should be evidenced in their level of creativity.

21 MORE DIRECTING, LESS DESIGNING

'Before you are a leader, success is all about growing yourself. When you become a leader, success is about growing others.'

JACK WELCH

What Is the Rule?

Contributing your own design work to the creative process may be necessary from time to time, but recognise that you may be directly 'competing' with your team. Some but not all of your designers may interpret your actions in this way because they have no control over the design selection decision, whereas you do. This could make them feel demotivated because you are taking away their creative freedom and the opportunity for their work to shine through. If you have the available resources, and it is an option, it may be more beneficial to maintain distance from projects and concentrate on directing the creative work of your team. Ultimately, this might preserve balance and help to produce the greatest creative output.

The Problem

In this scenario, the problem arises when you select your own design work over that of your team. Your design work may very well be the strongest and the best option for the project. But how do you think your team will feel seeing you select your own designs over their contributions? It might be the 'correct' decision in design terms, but understand that there are psychological consequences which can have a longer-term impact on the creative output of the design function. The more emotional characters in your team might struggle with this situation as it will knock their confidence and discourage them. Having been through this myself, I know it is a difficult situation to avoid because the very best design work must always be selected. I believe in a creative environment where ideas win on merit, regardless of who generates them. All design work should be considered as belonging to the 'team' as group ownership helps to avoid conflicts of ego and individual control over projects. However, as leader, becoming too regularly immersed in the 'doing' of the design creation can cause tensions to arise.

The Solution

Remaining more detached from the execution of design work will help you to maintain objectivity. You'll have a bird's eye view of each project which will be more informed and acute. It will also mean your team will perceive you as a neutral and guiding leader able to make robust decisions. You will benefit the team by empowering them and stepping back from the execution of the details, demonstrating your trust in their work. In directing rather than designing, you will be doing a better job as a creative leader.

You will also benefit from not having to balance design execution with design management activities. Juggling both responsibilities is not straightforward because management involves critical planning, which is just as important and urgent as design work on ongoing projects. Ideally, both activities should be happening at the same time.

Consider the following aspects when directing your team's creative work:

• Instead of taking on design work yourself, check in with the designers and discuss and direct suggested tweaks or builds to design work for further exploration. You can still sketch 'with' the designer and share suggestions, but in this capacity, you will be supporting them rather than taking control. You can steer them in what you understand intuitively to be the right direction based on your knowledge, skills and experience. This will leave the designer feeling happy, supported and motivated. They will be driven to be more productive because they feel they have more ownership and choice within the process.

• If it is necessary to select your own design work over that of the team, make the rationale for your choice very clear with parameters that align with answering the original design brief. This should help you to objectively demonstrate why your design work was required in this case so they feel reassured it won't happen every time.

• If you have a large team, suggest that this approach is followed by your other design managers so there is consistency across the whole design department.

Drawing It All Together

Focus on your role as design leader – this is what you've been hired to do. Although it might be tempting to keep your hand in by working on the day-to-day design detail of projects, it's not just a waste of your managerial time; it can seriously undermine the confidence, motivation and output of your designers if they feel you are competing with them rather than supporting and nurturing them. Concentrate on helping them to grow rather than stepping in to take control. Ultimately, this will mean you become a better leader and your team will produce better creative outputs.

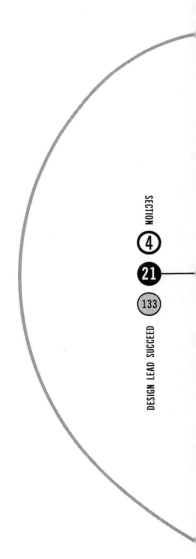

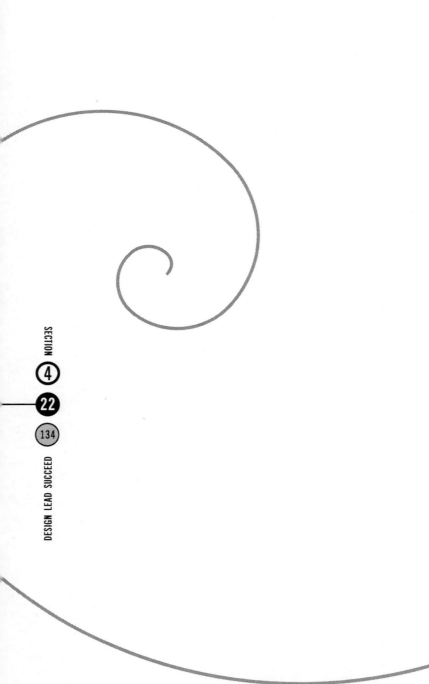

22 MANAGE YOUR AND YOUR TEAM'S TIME

'Planning is bringing the future into the present so that you can do something about it now.'

ALAN LAKEIN

What Is the Rule?

Time is one of your most valuable assets and it's within your control. Your ability to effectively manage the time you have available will dictate whether you succeed or fail as a design leader.

The Problem

One of the biggest issues you'll face as a design leader is fulfilling the expectations of the organisation for delivering new projects within the time required for market launch. There will always be a race against the clock, and you will always have to find ways to work more efficiently as an individual and as a team. If you can streamline your activities and manage time carefully, you will thrive.

But 'time' is not an isolated variable. Within the design creation process, time is linked to cost and quality of projects. The longer you take to produce, the more expensive the project will be. However, the faster you create, the more likely that quality will suffer. There will be a balancing point for you to judge on any project. If a project duration is too short to allow for the necessary quality of design work to be done, this invariably results in an inferior end result. Therefore, solutions to this issue need to be proposed. If time cannot be increased, you perhaps need to bring in more designers, but this pushes up project cost. This interplay of the components of time, cost and quality is complex, but it must be interrogated and resolved so that brand reputation and budgets aren't undermined.

All phases of a design project are very important, but from experience, giving enough time for design research at the beginning, before ideation has started, is critical! The time needed for the research phase of a new product will vary, but it is important that this period of work is protected and carried out. Without it there may be a lack of new insights or new ways of understanding the problem, and it's new insights which could lead to novel and unique solutions. For example, while working within an innovation team, I carried out research into how products fitting the face could be made more comfortable. Our research led us to try interesting methods such as head scanning to better understand the ergonomics. It allowed us to define a head shape which represented the average consumer. We then developed ergonomic design tools which led to the creation of products with market-leading levels of comfort and fit. Without the time allocated for design research, this result would not have been possible.

The Solution

How you manage your personal time and your team's time will have a critical effect on your success as a design leader. Effective time management begins with you, and you need to be self-disciplined enough to secure enough of your own personal time each week for creative planning purposes. This will allow you to look far into the future and forecast opportunities and threats to your team and projects. For example, a threat might be a lack of design resources due to the overlap of scheduled team member holidays. You can shape the team's attitude to timelines, but you should also consider giving project management responsibilities to members of your team so they can help you to keep timelines on track.

Careful management and communication of timelines, both with your team and with other teams in the organisation, is critical for success. Consider the following aspects when looking to implement effective time management:

Internal management and communication of timelines
- Build in a 20% buffer when creating the timelines for design projects. This generally allows for the unforeseen issues which often arise.
- Understand how different individuals in the team prefer to read and use timelines and then provide them in the variety of preferred formats for ease of reference.
- Make timelines physical and visible in the design studio. Digital timelines are not always referred to as they're not as easily accessible.
- Because timelines often change on a daily basis, make sharing of timelines a regular occurrence.

- Make sure everyone in the team is aware of timelines by regularly referring to deadlines in weekly team and project meetings.

External management and communication of timelines
- Define and stick to project timelines. It is not good to let deadlines slip as it leads to the design function gaining a poor reputation for late delivery.
- Design time for you and your team needs to be protected for the most creative results. There needs to be sufficient time built in to find the undiscovered insights which make new products original. There is often a misconception among those who are not creatives about how quickly creative design can be generated. Many functions outside of design might believe that a magic button exists on a computer within the design office. By simply pressing this button, the new design solution magically pops out! You need to be able to demonstrate how important this time is and secure it for your team. For example, you could illustrate the design process with a case study to show them how much work is involved.
- Building timelines with external functions is critical because design activities are only one part of the process of bringing a product to market. Often the 'bottleneck' or delay to the process may be caused by a team outside of design who have fewer resources. Ideally, your organisation will have project managers assigned to key business projects who can help to coordinate this collaboration between teams.
- Manage business expectations early on if there is a problem. For example, a high workload and insufficient design resources may mean a delay is inevitable. As a great design manager I once worked with used to say, 'No one shoots the messenger, unless the message is late!'

Assigning project management responsibilities
- Train up designers within your team to have a competent level of project management understanding and familiarity with working principles.
- The larger the organisation, project or components of the design, the higher the complexity and the greater the need for project management. Large projects require a clearly visible critical path of control. In a larger design team, you will find it hard to manage the timelines for every team project, so appoint a project manager or design operations manager with responsibility for overseeing all projects within the design function. Depending on the size of your team, they could be termed a 'programme manager' if they are overseeing multiple projects.
- Implement appropriate project management software which integrates into the design process and the wider organisation. This will help the whole team to keep abreast of how projects are progressing, contributing to clear communication and greater levels of productivity.

DESIGN LEAD SUCCEED

Drawing It All Together

Your success or failure as a design leader hinges on how well you manage time. This valuable asset cannot be put on pause like other assets at your disposal. It needs to be immediately managed and managed well! Managing time effectively means being disciplined and effectively allocating responsibilities for time and project management within the design team; it also means controlling how the team activities link up with the other functions in the organisation.

But critically, it is also about securing enough time for design research activities at the beginning of any project. This is essential for harvesting new insights which will elevate the design of any product and increase the value of your design project.

23 DIRECT THROUGH DESIGN BRIEFS

'You can't be lost on a straight road.'
PROVERB

What Is the Rule?

Design briefs are not just another administrative burden in an already busy creative process; they're an invaluable opportunity for a design leader to monitor and control the direction and progress of the design team. Defining a vision of the future, the design brief sets a path for the team to navigate a project from start to finish.

The Problem

While leading a design function, you may have numerous ongoing projects in progress. Without some sort of design brief for each project, there will be ambiguity and uncertainty around when it has reached its intended goal and the standard you are looking for. Many new products have failed because of poor planning and the lack of a clear design brief from the outset.

The Solution

The design brief spreads a layer of objectivity over the subjective practice of design creation. Once you have approved its contents, you will have peace of mind and confidence that the team are working in the correct manner and to the correct standards.

Another benefit is that it provides a quick and easy tool to bring new stakeholders up to speed and into a project. They can read the brief and quickly grasp the challenge, which then helps them to understand where they fit and how they can contribute and add value.

Consider the following aspects when setting up and signing off design briefs:

Choose an intuitive design brief template – It improves communication between teams and individuals if the design brief template uses a commonly recognised visual format with agreed terminology because it becomes more intuitive and easier to navigate. Where a design brief is provided by a client, it is advisable to develop this into the familiar template used by the design team.

Highlight the objective – Begin with a clear objective on the first page which communicates the purpose and value of the project to the team. This should have specific details about its alignment with the business strategy and how it can contribute to that.

Assign ownership – The design brief should be owned and created by the project manager – either the lead design manager or a designer on the project – from a neutral business standpoint. Neutrality allows for more objectivity in decisions, meaning they are based on the best interests of the business rather than being biased towards one particular individual or team's agenda. They should also have responsibility for updating it when required.

Provide certainty – Defining what is inside and outside of the scope of the project helps to reduce uncertainty for everyone and increase their focus on the task at hand.

Make it a visible 'living' document – When the brief is finished, keep it visible and close at hand. Have it available for reference in all meetings. Don't let it get out of date – it is a 'living' document that must reflect reality if it is to be useful. If the goal posts change on a project, the owner will need to update the plan and all the associated aspects such as budget, timelines and quality.

Maintain a level of control – Applying a final approval stage to any design brief, before it goes live, helps you to maintain your control over the contents to ensure it is aligned with your vision and that of the business.

Drawing It All Together

As the design leader, it's your responsibility to reinforce the necessity for the creation of and regular reference to clearly defined design briefs. They serve as invaluable navigation tools as you move through the design creation process. Crucially, as the design leader, you must also step back and assess how many design briefs are being assigned to your team. Be on guard for situations in which the company has initiated too many projects for the resources available. There should be a system in place for prioritising which design briefs are the most important for the business to progress. In these situations, it is your job to recognise the problem and suggest recommended courses of action, including which design briefs to fast track and which to pause.

DESIGN LEAD SUCCEED

24 GUIDE YOUR TEAM WITH THE MARKETING CLAIMS

'Marketing without design is lifeless.
Design without marketing is mute.'

VON GLITSCHKA

What Is the Rule?

It's one thing to suggest that your product and marketing communications must align seamlessly, but it's another trying to do this in reality. Without clear alignment and agreement on marketing claims between the design and marketing teams at the beginning of the creative process, there'll be an obvious disconnect between the words and the style of your product. As a consequence, the consumer won't feel as emotionally drawn to your offering, although they won't realise the reason why.

The Problem

If the marketing claim for your product is: 'Lightweight and superior comfort', then your product needs to visually communicate this statement in the way it's styled and constructed as well as in how it functions. If the product looks markedly different to the descriptive words on the packaging and the look and feel of the advertising campaign, then the consumer will be confused. If they're confused, they'll hesitate in choosing your product over competitors' products in the same aisle. The implications of this disconnect are clearly huge. The problem is not only in aligning the words and the visuals, but in aligning the design and marketing teams behind a common cause.

The Solution

The best way to ensure that there's a seamless, continuous connection between the marketing campaign's words and the product is to embed these words into the design creation process from the very beginning of the project. As the design leader, you should work hard on building a strong, trusting relationship with your marketing counterpart within the organisation. Moreover, you should work together to cultivate fully-integrated working practices during the design creation process between the functions of design and marketing. Agree with the marketing team what the claims regarding features of the product could be when launched. As long as you agree that this summarises the story of the product, use it.

Hang the claims high on the studio wall for all to see and understand. It's equally important as the project plan. And here's the crux: use it as a filter and as parameters when reviewing any concept designs with the team. Use it like a question in every review that the whole team can use to interrogate decisions. Use it in design reviews to create the criteria for fulfilling the brief. This laser focus on the claim description speeds up the design creation process, keeping the team on track and preventing any creative deviations or tangents.

For example, you could be creating a sports watch. The brand and the product strapline is: 'Rugged and built to last a lifetime'. A powerful thing happens when you introduce this phrase to the concept review. It cuts through all subjective opinion. It instantly refreshes all those present on the focussed goal of the product. It makes the decision process easier in filtering concepts and selecting one over another. It helps to direct the team in how a chosen concept could be improved and what could be added. Very simply, the chosen concept should look 'rugged' and 'strong'. This can be achieved through the use of physical form, surfaces, materials, surface finishes and colour.

This strapline can also be used to great effect externally; for example, in presentations to wider teams, retailers and buyers. It allows the story and purpose of the product to be captured in a sentence.

Drawing It All Together

Your product will only resonate with consumers if the design is aligned with the messaging, and this can only occur if there is cohesion between the design and marketing functions at the inception of the product and throughout the design creation process. The marketing claims, which serve to highlight the key features and benefits of the product to the consumer, are also a guiding light for the design team during the creative process to help maintain focus on these consumer pain points.

25 SHEPHERD IDEAS TOWARDS SOLUTIONS

'You hope to produce a classic...You can refine something forever, but you reach a point where you're going backwards.'

WARREN PLATNER

What Is the Rule?

Navigating the creative process as a leader involves shepherding your team's ideas towards a final chosen solution. But this process isn't linear or straightforward. Design exploration involves a journey of repeated phases of 'diverging' and 'converging'. When diverging, you are encouraging expansion of the number of ideas so as to cultivate creativity and explore the breadth of solutions available. When converging, you are filtering down to the best solutions through a process of analysis and learning. Being aware of your tendency to either naturally diverge or converge ideas as a leader, and improving your abilities in both, will help you to effectively manage the design creation process and the team of creatives and, ultimately, capitalise on more opportunities, resulting in better outputs.

The Problem

As leader of the creation process, you are responsible for managing individuals, teams and projects and allowing only the very best ideas to win through in the end. You must lead the cyclical process of testing ideas, learning and then redesigning with improvements. This may include multiple iterations of feedback loops as you move ever closer to the often fixed and immovable project deadline. Classic design innovation theory describes the journey of ideation as starting with many initial ideas (diverging), which then pass through a funnel, narrowing down the options (converging), and eventually leading to a final chosen product concept. Generally, from experience, the more feedback loops you have, the greater the opportunity to improve a design and make it successful.

But you must balance this desire to ensure the design is refined in this way with the need to hit your schedule. The diverging and converging phases occur within each one of these feedback cycles and managing them well is essential to successfully refining the design and hitting the launch date.

There are some key issues to consider around divergence and convergence when leading and managing design creation. These need to be considered at the individual and team project level:

Leading the team – When leading and in design management activities, you must be careful not to converge too quickly and narrow down a project to a conclusion if there is still sufficient time to diverge and iterate to discover further variants. On the other hand, if you prefer to diverge as a leader, constantly looking for other options, it might mean that the whole project will be late and fail as a result.

Leading individuals – As individuals, we tend to have natural preferences. Some people will naturally always want to diverge and explore as many different ideas as possible. This is a great instinct for a designer, but enough time needs to be allocated for converging and refining an idea. If someone doesn't stop brainstorming ideas and fails to whittle them down towards a solution, deadlines are missed and ideas are insufficiently resolved. As a design leader, this presents a problem. On the flip side, if a designer is naturally able to converge their ideas at the right point in the process, it helps them to make progress, and their work will be much easier to shepherd, as long as they've still produced a sufficient breadth of ideas from which to develop a strong creative route forward.

The Solution

Try to discover your default personal approach to diverging and converging and improve your skills in both so as to find the right balance.

Knowing yourself and managing the team

This begins by trying to consciously recognise your past and present behaviour in situations. Proficiency in both diverging and converging is essential, but you may be more talented or naturally lean to one over the other during the creative process. I know that I can both diverge and converge as a designer and leader. However, over time I've discovered that, as a design leader, I may have been converging the team projects a little too early in my eagerness to shift designers and resource across to other urgent projects. Because of this, we hit deadlines, but I wonder if

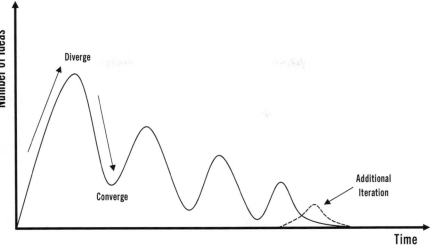

Figure 25.1 Diverging and converging during the design creation process

further divergence could have produced another quick iteration of ideas or a specific design feature for further refinement, as outlined in Figure 25.1. In that haste to make sure that an important target is met, you may ignore a golden opportunity to explore a detail which could alter the direction of the project and make it even stronger. To find the best solution, you need to be able to converge but then be prepared to diverge again if an opportunity arises.

Managing individuals

Managing individuals in the team also needs to be considered if morale and motivation is to be maintained. As the design leader, you need to be aware of the naturally-favoured approaches of each person. There will be individuals who naturally wish to diverge a lot. Do not restrict them too much by converging too quickly, and be conscious to allow them ample opportunity to explore. Give them the space because they may surprise you with what they achieve. Conversely, challenge the individual who is quick to rest upon a solution and who naturally converges. Prompt them to interrogate their design rationale and how it could be improved.

Drawing It All Together

It's not always easy to choose the right way forward as a leader, but you need to be able to make the critical decisions and shepherd your team's ideas towards the sharp end of the funnel. It's all about finding a balance between exploring ideas and filtering them down, something that can happen in multiple cycles before a final choice is made. This is like panning for gold – recognising the opportunities available to you through divergence and convergence at key moments. Learn to use your 'feel' and experience as a leader to recognise when these pivot points arise in the process and when it is best to diverge or converge.

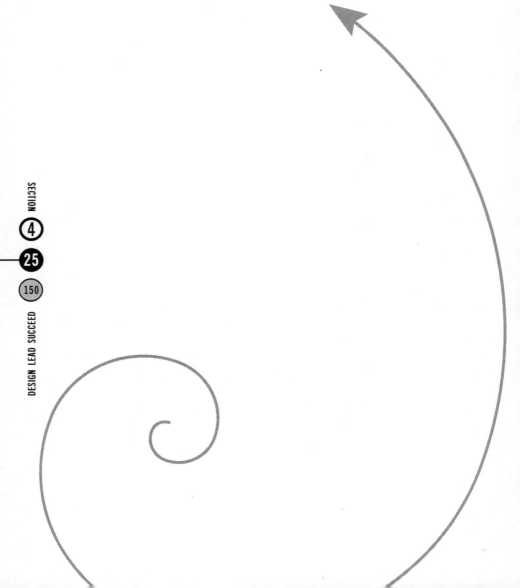

26 UTILISE DESIGN REVIEWS FOR QUALITY CONTROL

'Good design is thorough down to the last detail. Nothing must be arbitrary or left to chance. Care and accuracy in the design process show respect towards the user.'

DIETER RAMS

What Is the Rule?

As the design leader, you need to test developing ideas and outputs to check whether they are appropriate in relation to the design brief (tracking the project time, cost and quality). You're not involved in every detail of every project, but by approving work within design reviews, you maintain a clear view and control over the situation as well as the standard of all outputs that leave your department. This, ultimately, is what will protect your reputation for design excellence.

The Problem

The challenge, as a design leader, is to ensure high-quality and relevant design work is repeatedly created by your team. But design reviews can often be seen by designers as micro-management that goes over old ground; they might perceive them as an unnecessary chore requiring too much preparation. But without them, the design work can progress unchecked and with inherent errors, wasting time further down the line when it needs to be corrected at the end of the project or causing problems when the product goes out to market.

In larger design teams, with so many projects ongoing, it becomes vital for you to build reviews into the process in order to evaluate your design outputs. Depending on the size of your team, the review may be one of the few times that some designers receive your direct input and guidance.

The Solution

The ISO 9001:2008 standard for 'quality management systems' offers a great basis for how to set up and structure reviews during the design and development of products.

Section 7.3.4, *'Design and development review'*, suggests suitable staged reviews during design development should be carried out 'a) to evaluate the ability of the results of design and development to meet requirements', and 'b) to identify any problems and propose necessary actions'. The standard also suggests that participants in the reviews include representatives from the relevant functions involved in the design and development of the product and that records of the results of the reviews with agreed actions should be maintained.

The International Organisation for Standardisation (ISO) was founded in 1947 because of the need for greater levels of consumer confidence in terms of product safety, reliability and quality, especially in the medical or aerospace industries, for example, where lives are at risk. Among other things, they've developed international standards for the best way of creating products. Not only do the standards act as guidance to industry practitioners, but they are also relied upon by governments and regulators to help develop better regulation because they are formulated by groups of international experts.

Consider the following points when setting up and carrying out design reviews for the best possible results:

Preparing for the design review

Be clear about the purpose – It's important to clearly define the purpose of the design review within the agreed agenda of the meeting so that all involved are clear on the expected outcomes.

Ensure you have the right attendees – You should confirm the attendance of those who contribute to the decision-making process and approvals in advance of the design review, otherwise the meeting will be a waste of time because the outcomes won't be achievable. It is usual for the project manager to attend design reviews where appointed.

Schedule early in the day – Mental focus is greater in the morning when people are fresh and rested. So, for greater engagement and quality of decision-making, try to schedule design reviews before lunchtime.

Define expectations – To aid the smooth flow of the design review, request that specific design details and aspects of concern for your approval or sign-off be provided in advance. And ensure that they are presented to you with recommended solutions, including a clear rationale and evidence. Other documents typically considered at the design review would include the design brief and project plan or program.

Review design work first – When a design review includes other business functions and acts as a later stage gateway for the product, review the design work internally first. Again, this aids the smooth running of the meeting because it ensures that you, as design leader, are happy and satisfied with the quality of the proposed design work and the full design team is aligned and clear on the approach before it's presented to the wider company.

Balance the number of design reviews – As the design leader, it's important to always be conscious of getting the balance right between too few and too many design reviews. We've already discussed the risk of too few, but too many could potentially suck up valuable design creation time. Ultimately, this will come down to your intuition. But projects with less experienced designers or those that are most important in terms of value to the business may require more design reviews.

Carrying out the design review

Ask for recommendations – Always request a recommendation from the design team as to what they believe the best solution is and what the best next step is, backed up by a clear rationale and compelling data. They are closer to the details of the project, and this approach helps to speed up the review by distilling all their thoughts into a concise argument for discussion.

Welcome broader input – Design reviews allow more eyes on the problem from different functions. This approach will ultimately lead to a stronger result because of greater integration of the design proposals, helping to minimise any weaknesses that exist in the overall design of the product.

Hear from all design specialisms – It's beneficial to remind review attendees to listen to and respect the comments and suggestions from all the different design subject specialisms. This ensures that all views and concerns are aired. As leader, you can then take more informed decisions by synthesising these with your own knowledge and the wider business context for the project.

Make decisions at the right time – Sometimes, the intended goal of a review cannot be achieved because there's not enough information available or the necessary quality of work still hasn't been produced. Don't be afraid to action the additional work and reschedule another review.

Assign a note taker – Always assign a member of the team with responsibility for note taking and capturing actions during the design review. It's best that this isn't you as the design leader because you need to be listening intently throughout and fully engaged in all of the discussions.

Record next steps – When the review has concluded, ensure that the decisions, approvals and next steps have been summarised.

Drawing It All Together

As the design leader, it's critical that you're able to maintain design excellence in the creation process. The insertion of design reviews allows you to assert your control, influence and authority, providing approval and final sign-off on all project work. These reviews should be valued and capitalised on as significant landmarks for design assessment and occasions for social bonding among the team. They're an opportunity for you, as leader, to share praise for accomplishments and progress but also to provide necessary critical analysis if expectations are not being met.

27 LOOK BACK, LEARN AND THEN LEAP FORWARD

'We do not learn from experience, we learn from reflecting on experience.'

JOHN DEWEY

What Is the Rule?

Schedule regular sessions to pause and reflect on performance during and after the completion of creative projects. These reviews will allow you and your team to learn quickly and move forwards stronger and more productively than ever before.

The Problem

If completed design projects are not reviewed and the sequence of events is not dissected afterwards, then any issues and mistakes which may have occurred will continue to occur. Indeed, they could potentially grow in terms of their negative impact on the creative potential and speed of any future project. The goal should be to streamline any project design activities by breaking down any barriers you experienced and building new approaches if necessary. From past experience, the most common issues tend to be around IT systems, design hardware and software supporting the creation process and communication between individuals and groups of people on projects.

Of course, urgent issues which risk the very existence of a project will need to be dealt with during the process rather than after completion, but many other problematic issues can remain unidentified in the moment, or identified but tolerated. Many of these are easier to assess once the project has been completed and everyone has had a chance to reflect on what happened. At this point, there can be a process of stepping back from the situation and understanding how the event unfolded in a more objective manner. Naturally, the rigorous recording of issues throughout a project is essential for performance reviews to be effective.

The Solution

Reviewing any past design project can be a cathartic experience for your team. It offers them a safe space where they can share frustrations, feel listened to and collectively contribute to ideas for improvements and resolutions of problematic issues. Create an environment based on trust for the review session where the focus is on honesty and learning with no finger pointing and blame. The purpose of the session must be group improvement. The truth will not come out if people do not feel safe enough to share their experiences and potential learnings.

Consider the following aspects when organising the sessions:

• **Start with a warm-up exercise** – Begin the session with a warm-up exercise, such as an ice-breaker question, as a way of getting the conversation flowing.

• **Encourage respect and participation** – Importantly, reiterate at the beginning of the session that no idea or suggestion should be considered stupid or dismissed by anyone. Respect should be maintained at all times.

• **Include the whole project team** – This will ensure there is maximum buy-in in terms of the issues outlined for improvement and the required actions.

• **Consider ideation techniques** – Techniques such as the Six Thinking Hats can be an excellent approach because it captures the perceived positive and negative facts, opinions and emotions of the individuals in the session. This encourages an objective categorising of all the events and variables so that patterns of recurring issues and single-case issues can be identified and prioritised in terms of their future risk and impact to the team's working practices.

• **Ask three critical questions** – As a starting point, ask these three critical questions: 'What went well?', 'What did not go well?' and, 'What would we do differently next time?' These lines of inquiry can be efficient in quickly identifying and resolving issues, especially in shorter sessions. I adopted and adapted this approach after attending a lecture by the RAF Red Arrows display team at Nottingham University one evening. This is how they quickly assessed their performance after every flight in order to improve their next performance. They also promote a 'culture of excellence' where individuals are commended for admitting errors so that the team can learn quickly and improve for the next flight.

• **Direct questions to everyone** – Facilitate the session in a way which allows time for every individual to contribute and to be listened to by directing questions around the room.

• **Reflect on the risks** – It's also worth exploring project risks as well as actual issues. What could have gone wrong? Risks turn into issues in the future, so this helps you to prevent future problems.

• **Take the temperature** – Conclude the session by requesting that each individual cite at least three 'most important' issues. This enables a temperature test of the room to ascertain what the team see as the biggest problems. You will also find that if you resolve the most identified issues, you will win the room.

• **Record the key issues** – Transcribing the issues for improvement in real time during the session provides a visual reference for the whole group to build on. This also helps to focus the continuous flow of the discussion and avoids the problem of the same issue being repeatedly discussed by the group. This can often be a problem if a discussion is held purely as a verbal interaction with no visual props. Once the issues are documented, prioritise each point and assign responsibility for resolving them.

• **Share the session notes** – Circulate these promptly with the group afterwards so that points can be added and there is the opportunity for them to come up with additional ideas for resolving issues. As leader, you should be transparent about which issues will be tackled and in which order. Their notes can remain anonymous, however, and you can make this clear to the team, which should give them more freedom to share ideas and opinions.

• **Conduct reviews with individuals** – These are as important as team reviews. This will help to pull out learnings that some may feel uncomfortable sharing in a group setting.

• **Follow up on progress** – After the review, follow up with those responsible for making the improvements and track the resolution of the prioritised issues. Share these outcomes with the team so they feel involved in the process, confident in your leadership and buoyed by the progress you're making. Knowing they are being supported to reach their performance standards will motivate them as a team.

• **Engage with other functions** – Many issues which arise are connected to and affected by other functions within the organisation, so engage with other functional leaders to make improvements and even schedule collective improvement reviews.

Drawing It All Together

Dedicating time to revisiting past projects as a team is an extremely powerful tool for improvement. Honest and open sharing of individual mistakes can be pivotal in discovering team blind spots. By reiterating the value and purpose of the review, you can defuse any potential conflict or anxiety around it and galvanise the team's desire to make progress and develop. Whether the reviews are held frequently or after longer projects, by taking the opportunity to come together as a team, it will help to significantly raise the level of future performance and team morale.

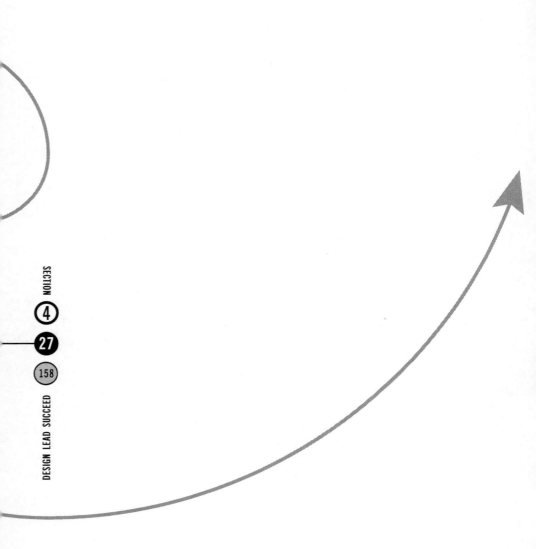

28 SEARCH FOR SIMPLICITY

'Like a sculptor building a statue, not by adding, but by hacking away the unessential so that the truth will be revealed unobstructed.'

BRUCE LEE

What Is the Rule?

Being the design leader places you in a unique position to drive productivity by simplifying the work environment. The workplace is a highly complex place, and we have to constantly adapt to change and new challenges. With oversight of product creation and how processes, projects and people connect throughout your organisation, you are able to review and adjust practice at each crux point to ensure things are as straightforward and efficient as they can be.

The Problem

A leader's working day is highly complex, with many different issues to consider involving projects, people and business units. You have a finite amount of time in which to fit all these activities and they need to be prioritised appropriately for you to be effective in reaching your objectives. Bill Jensen, an expert in applying the principles of simplicity in business management, believes there is a common myth among business leaders that complexity in today's world arises from the fast-paced world 'out there'. We're told it's the marketplace and competitors that create the problem. But, in reality, he says, the number one cause of complexity in today's organisations is our failure to integrate change. If this problem isn't met head on, the product creation process could become more and more complex. It is your job to help unravel these complexities and identify the most direct route between one point and another.

DESIGN LEAD SUCCEED

From personal experience, each time my organisation altered course, there were subsequent changes to my team's structure and the wider functions, as well as different personnel and chains of command. It was important to respond by resetting and seeking to simplify the various existing design creation processes so that they remained effective and efficient within the new organisational set-up.

The Solution

Nature is the ultimate designer. If we look to nature as an example, we see that there is generally nothing superfluous or unnecessary. If a need in a species diminishes, then that body part will eventually waste away. What is redundant doesn't last long. Animals generally evolve into the simplest form necessary to meet the functional challenges of their environment. For example, evidence has been found to prove that the Brachymeles bicolor lizard from Southeast Asia evolved and dropped all four of its limbs around 62 million years ago to cope with a much drier environment. But then it grew its limbs back another 40 million years later as the environment and climate became wetter again.

Simplicity generates value, whether that's a reduction in time or costs, an increase in productivity or an improvement in product quality or consumer experience. For example, I've often found that when manufacturing in another city or country, the best way to simplify the process of working with the manufacturers is to eschew complex email chains and multiple conference calls and instead have one face-to-face meeting with the production engineers. This can significantly reduce the timeline of a project as it ensures clear communication and understanding between all parties from the word go. Importantly, simplicity also helps us improve our wellbeing, as a complex environment is a stressful environment.

Here are a few ideas for seeking out simplicity at the various levels of your design leadership role:

Organisation level

• There will always be changes occurring in organisations, whether they are structural or process-based. Inevitably, these events require time and energy, but they also open up opportunities to simplify working practices. Make the most of these moments. For example, consider how technology can help simplify processes through automation of repetitive tasks and data analysis. Map out the design function stakeholders and define what meetings are strictly necessary.

Process level

• Utilise naming conventions and methodology for documentation and physical sample archiving. These standardised procedures may be interpreted by some designers as unnecessary administrative work, but this approach makes for quicker identification and recall of documented information by any member of the team.

Project level

• When a new project is proposed, ask questions to ascertain if it should exist in the first place. For example, does the project support the objectives and strategy of the business and its criteria for return on investment in terms of building brand equity?
• Design reviews should always have clear objectives; they should produce recommended solutions to be reviewed and the approver should be in attendance. Otherwise, they are not producing the results required.
• All project meetings should have a clear purpose and agenda before they are approved.

Product level

• If your creation has unnecessary elements, then it will be more costly than it needs to be. Making things simpler not only makes the product work better but also delights the user.

Personal level

• Consider whether all meetings you attend are necessary or whether attendance can be delegated.
• Try to collate all of your design management tools into one place and one document so information is quick and easy to find. Simplicity brings speed and clarity of judgement.
• Minimise unnecessary communication by defining who needs to be CC'ed in on certain message types.
• Always ask yourself whether the information from several documents can be combined into one. Are you starting a new document when an existing one can incorporate that information?
• The question of how to simplify your daily workload through greater efficiencies could form the basis of an entire book. But regardless of the activity you are undertaking, you should always remember to continually ask yourself how it can be simplified. How can parts be reduced? How can parts be removed altogether? This simple concept should always be front of mind.

I'll give you one final example from my own life of a small change which simplified my working day. Post-it Notes are great tools, especially for ideation sessions, but while under pressure, during a busy day, I would often find myself frantically scribbling my actions onto Post-it Notes and attaching them to my screen or desk surface as reminders. The accumulation of a day's work would leave a messy array of random Post-its all over my workspace. Everyone has different working styles, but personally, I believe that a clean and minimal working space can help to focus the mind. The sight of all these Post-it Notes noticeably increased my stress levels. My solution has been to become more disciplined. Instead of using several Post-it Notes, I note down any actions in one place: an A5 notepad. There's no need to collate and rewrite a list at the end of the day. And the notepad can be closed and filed away before I exit the office, leaving a clean and uncluttered workspace.

Drawing It All Together

Search for simplicity in every level and element of your work. Constantly ask yourself, 'How could this be done more simply?', 'Is there a better way?' or 'Is there an alternative?' Simplicity improves productivity and increases your focus. But importantly, from a health and wellbeing perspective, it can also reduce your levels of stress and anxiety. Simplified and ordered tasks create structure and allow larger activities to be broken down into smaller steps. This helps to reduce multitasking and allows for a more focussed, single-minded approach.

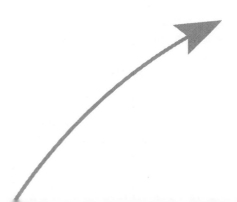

29 ESTABLISH OPERATIONAL EXCELLENCE

'The urge for good design is the same as the urge to go on living. The assumption is that somewhere, hidden, is a better way of doing things.'

HARRY BERTOIA

What Is the Rule?

A robust process allows a beautiful idea to fulfil its potential. Creating new, innovative and commercially successful products that can be produced repeatedly, to a high standard, is a hugely complex activity. The system that enables that needs to be operating seamlessly. This is why processes are important. They allow you to reduce time and costs and improve quality with each and every iteration you make. But you must also make sure that they don't become rigid and suffocating. It's a fine balance.

DESIGN LEAD SUCCEED

The Problem

Without a robust process, ideas and products would never come to fruition successfully and make money. But formal processes also have the potential to restrict creativity if they are too embedded and rigid. In his pioneering book *The Innovator's Dilemma*, Clayton Christensen suggests that processes can be inflexible and make it difficult for an organisation to be agile and change. This explains why market-leading companies sometimes find it harder to generate disruptive innovations which shake up industries and create paradigm shifts. Their more common breakthrough innovations are generally classified as improvements on an existing product.

This is because when an organisation is successful, it grows and becomes more operationally complex with more processes to meet rising demands. Understandably, once these processes are set up and embedded, it's going to be efficient and effective at delivering the current products for the organisation, but may hinder new and diverse creations with the potential to be game-changers. Alternatively, a start-up business can be lean and agile, able to build processes from scratch that are tailored for a new product it's creating.

The Solution

Processes can be formal or informal, and both types are essential for successful projects. The formal processes, such as documentation, set routines and procedures during the creative process, require discipline if they are to be used effectively. They improve productivity and free up valuable space and time for the designers' informal processes. These might be setting aside time for creative exploration and research. It is quite fitting that the word 'product' comes just after 'process' in the dictionary. To successfully create a product, there first needs to be a robust process in place and this should be a priority for you as the design leader. You also need to build design processes which will integrate into the wider organisation's processes, such as their product lifecycle management systems which hold all the product information necessary for manufacture.

But you must be careful in creating a design process; it should be robust but also flexible. You should seek balance so that you can capitalise on disruptive and breakthrough innovations. Creativity should be allowed to thrive, and administrative burdens on designers should be minimised to allow more time for exploration and creation.

Here are a number of steps you can take to start building operational excellence:

Assess what's already there

Whenever you're building a design team or joining an existing one, it's important to audit the current design operations and identify what processes currently exist. Distinguish whether they are design management, design operations or general business operation systems. This will help you to understand if there is too much or too little process.

Do regular reviews

An effective method of understanding how robust your processes are is to carry out quarterly team reviews of project work. Feedback from the team and outside functions will help to suggest if a process is operating smoothly or if it requires adjustment. Processes should act as enablers to enhance creativity and increase opportunities, by freeing up time for more design research for example. If you get feedback that the processes are creating problems or preventing team members from doing their work, remove them or change the system you're using. It's important to note that only documented processes are capable of effective review.

Delegate control of operations
Assign someone in your team to lead and execute the design operations activities. This will give them responsibility for continuous monitoring and control at a management and operational level, allowing you to step back a little from the detail of the day-to-day and gain greater perspective and clarity on what is working and what isn't. Moreover, some process activities should form part of every designer's workload. Assign leadership in specific areas of operation aligned with their talents, passions and areas for personal development.

Be disciplined
Depending on the type of process, it may be necessary to provide training to new team recruits and offer regular training updates to existing team members so that processes are followed correctly. For processes to work, they often require discipline from the participants so that inputs are correctly added. Otherwise, the process can't provide the benefits it promises. This requires a level of conformity and buy-in to the bigger picture and overall gains to the group.

Capture best practice on projects
People can leave your organisation at any time, taking all of their experience and working knowledge with them. The impact could be disastrous to a project, so it's a good idea to capture the informal processes adopted by your team members by asking them to create 'best practice' documents as they progress. They should briefly outline the required steps in any particular activity which they carry out on a project. This will help the organisation to hold on to the valuable tacit and cognitive knowledge held within your team and make it accessible to all future recruits.

Utilise automation to ensure consistency
There may be opportunities you can leverage by automating many of the manual design tasks to ensure consistency and bypass the time required to complete processes. For example, Python is an open-source programming language software which can be used to write scripts which automate repetitive design tasks.

Drawing It All Together

As the leader of your team, you must continuously seek operational excellence to reduce time and costs and improve quality and the potential for creativity. This can be aided by assigning team members to design operations roles. But ultimately, continued operational excellence should be a shared responsibility of search and discovery by every member of the team, and they should be encouraged to share their identified pain points and areas for potential improvement with the designated team members. This approach follows the Japanese business philosophy of 'Kaizen', meaning 'continuous improvement', where every employee is encouraged to share ideas that develop and refine processes at any time. And remember that although creativity needs to be based on a strong process, it pays to be wary of processes which become too rigid and inflexible, preventing you from adapting quickly to new or changing industry technologies, for example. So, seek balance. There needs to be an understanding that processes act as enablers to help enhance creativity and not to stifle it.

30 TAKE CHARGE OF YOUR FINANCIAL PLANNING

'Think ahead. Don't let day-to-day operations drive out planning.'

DONALD RUMSFELD

What Is the Rule?

Successful financial planning and daily execution of that plan underpins the smooth operation of your department. Clarity on your realms of financial responsibility and accountability will allow you to form annual budgets which allow for swift decision-making and smooth design execution.

The Problem

For a design department to operate smoothly, it needs people and materials as a minimum, and these incur running costs. The largest cost could be your permanent people, but there are also temporary people and external consultants. Your realms of financial control may vary depending on your company and design discipline, but you may also have accountability for the cost of manufacture. There will also be costs for design tools such as software and hardware which are essential for getting the best output from your design team.

Without a clear financial plan and visibility of the budget available to you and your department, you'll be in a weak position from which to lead and build success. Lack of clarity on this will mean you waste chunks of your time generating requests, building business cases to justify spending and waiting for approvals from the finance department. This reactive approach can also increase costs. For example, team travel costs can increase significantly if transport is booked at the last minute.

The Solution

Give the financial planning and budget for your department the time and focus that it needs. The core financial activities for any business involve creating an annual budget as well as predicting the costs of day-to-day operations, so plan ahead of the following year for what these needs will be. But also consider at least three years ahead, including how the budget may need to change and evolve over time.

Consider the following aspects for your financial planning and budget management activities:

• When asked to plan for 12 months, build it for three years. In this way, you can take account of progression and training and longer-term changes such as an increase in your team size.

• Start your planning process well in advance to ensure that you've covered every base and that you have the time to draw on multiple sources for input and advice.

• Include the team in the budgeting process and be as transparent as possible about available funds. This will build trust and motivation as they will feel they have some control and influence. It also helps them to appreciate the value of things and how to be frugal. If you have to make tough financial decisions, they'll better understand the reasoning behind them. You should also check your budget regularly with your design managers to make sure that projects are on track.

• Make sure that your financial plan aligns with the overall business strategy. You'll have a much higher chance of approval if they can see that your budget directly supports their goals. Make sure that you justify every expense you include so they have all they need to say 'yes'.

• Understand and keep abreast of the on-going costs of your team and overheads. This is a sobering process that will help you keep a sense of what value must be returned in your design output.

• Build a strong relationship with the finance team as they are your first point of contact and can easily slow down your progress. Their support underpins your success and a positive connection can speed up decision-making and approval of requests.

• Build business cases to request more when needed. If you're struggling to produce a quality product because of lack of funds, leadership will want you to flag this up.

• Leverage the financial reports of competitors to glean insights into how they balance their books and produce great products on a budget. This will help you to benchmark your own activities. For example, you can gauge how much your competitors are investing in research and development to generate new insights and technologies.

- Work with other teams and departments to share costs and combine your efforts in requests for more funding. Multiple requests take more time and effort, so you are simplifying the process. The more of you there are, the more compelling your case will be.
- Recognise the difference between good and bad investments. Use financial analysis methodologies – such as net present value and payback period – which help to illustrate the potential benefits of your investments in your business case requests. Ask your financial department colleagues for assistance here because they may use standard methodologies which are necessary for funding approvals in your organisation.
- Use the previous year's budget as a starting point for building your plan. This will help to dramatically speed up the process because you'll have a realistic baseline of what was actually spent, which can then be adjusted for the following year.

Drawing It All Together

Competent financial planning serves as the foundation for leading the smooth operation of your design department in the pursuit of building beautiful products. It's important to effectively manage the execution of your annual budget and always plan a few years ahead in order to become less reactive. It's also critical to build business cases which align with your business strategy, helping you to secure essential investment to grow the capabilities of your team.

PROTECT YOUR TEAM IN RELATION TO INTELLECTUAL PROPERTY

'Mountains are not fair or unfair - they are dangerous.'

REINHOLD MESSNER

What Is the Rule?

In a world where originality is becoming harder and harder to achieve, it would be naïve not to check whether you have accidentally infringed an existing patent or design registration. Conversely, it's critical to protect the intellectual property (IP) you generate. This serves as evidence of the value your team creates and potentially protects future revenue streams for your business.

The Problem

There is an ever-present risk of patent infringement in design. If you inadvertently infringe an existing patent, the consequences could be severe. According to the American Intellectual Property Law Association, litigation costs average in excess of $3 million where the amount being disputed is between $1 million and $25 million. And even in cases where the amount in dispute is less than $1 million, in some instances, litigation costs may exceed the amount at stake. There are also 'patent trolls' that are ready to pounce. These are owners of patents that lie dormant, waiting for someone to infringe them so they can sue. They may hold the patents but they're often not actually using them on a product in existence. Mitigating the risk of inadvertently infringing existing IP should be considered a key focus for any company as the consequences are potentially huge in terms of litigation costs and loss of reputation.

On the flip side, the ideas and designs that you create should be protected as your 'intellectual property' to maintain your competitive advantage in your market and to better exploit your organisation's investment in research and development.

There is discussion around the notion that patent protection stifles innovation as it prevents the natural process of exploration in design, which can sometimes rely on combining ideas from different parties working together. However, a good argument in favour of patents is that it protects the inventor for 20 years, giving them a monopoly for a period which allows them to make a financial success of their design. This means there's an incentive to invent. If there was no incentive, innovation may not provide as much economic growth.

The Solution

First, protect your ideas! Whether you need to apply for ownership of your idea depends on a number of factors. It's always advisable to seek the advice of an expert in this area such as a patent attorney. The amount you'll pay for protection will depend on how wide an area of the world you need to protect your idea in and the duration of time you intend to maintain the protection for. If you're successful, you will be granted ownership of the idea in specific regions of the world in the form of patents or design registrations. The management of your intellectual property shouldn't be considered an administrative burden but rather an opportunity to capitalise on the intellectual capital of your team and organisation. This allows you to maximise the benefits of your competitive advantage in the market.

Now consider how to avoid patent infringement. As a starting point, it's always advisable to carry out a 'prior art search' during the design creation process when you have your final working design developed. A patent attorney can then run a check to try and understand if your idea already exists. If it does, it'll mean you'll need to change your design in order to avoid infringing someone else's patent. Also, bear in mind that you'll never be 100% certain that you haven't accidently infringed someone's idea because pending patents don't have to be published and made publicly available, so they won't always show up on the results of a prior art search.

It's not always easy to avoid patent infringements and protect your intellectual property. It takes ongoing effort. Consider the following approaches to help reduce the risks:

Encourage a low-risk company culture

The actions and behaviours of individual employees and managers within an organisation can affect the level of risk exposure, so try to encourage a low-risk culture when it comes to IP. For example, designers can help to avoid accidently creating concepts which are already in the market by carrying out thorough competitor brand and product research. Preventative systems and processes can also help to direct appropriate behaviour and decisions. As Lang suggests, a system of documenting invention concepts on a daily basis should be implemented to provide vital evidence should proof of entitlement to a patent be required to negate someone else's claim.

Design around existing patents

As Lunn and Gilson describe, any product or process must demonstrate novelty in order to be patentable, or it must be sufficiently differentiated from an existing patent in order to be considered as 'not infringing'. Designing around the existing patents of competitors is therefore a task constantly faced by designers, and it might be a good approach as it allows you to make the process more straightforward. If you know what products you might infringe, you can keep them in mind and use them as hard parameters for your own design.

Create a company patent strategy

A company patent strategy helps to reduce the risk of patent infringement because it makes the topic a central component of the overall business strategy. It creates buy-in, visibility and understanding of its value in the senior leadership team. It's worth assigning responsibility to an individual for delivering the strategy and managing the organisation's 'patent portfolio'. Patent portfolios, the groups of patents owned by the business, can represent the major value of a larger firm's assets. They help maintain competitive advantage for the organisation but they also demonstrate proof of intellectual property and, in some situations, can serve as a defensive measure against claims of infringement from other businesses.

Monitor the competition and non-practising entities (NPEs)

By consistently reviewing and monitoring prior art, third-party and patent pending applications, as well as competitors' patent portfolios, you can keep abreast of the likely risks you'll encounter in patent infringement. It's good practice to implement patent search programs to regularly monitor issued patents from relevant competitors and non-practising entities where there may be a higher potential risk of patent infringement. Non-practising entities are owners who amass patents without the intention of using them. When they assert their ownership rights and claim infringement, they then become the aforementioned 'patent trolls'. Common methods of monitoring patent activity include hiring the help of patent attorneys, searching publicly available patent records and using patent search databases.

Get patent infringement insurance

Insurance is the most obvious risk management device available. Types of insurance available may include litigation insurance and net loss insurance. However, this is merely a defensive approach as it would only protect the individual or company from the financial losses if patent infringement occurred rather than preventing it altogether.

Cooperate with competitors

Cooperation across R&D departments in different firms is actually a common phenomenon in today's world, helping to increase the value of IP as well as reducing the risk of patent infringement. For example, it can help to reduce the risk of attack by 'patent trolls' as businesses can share their experiences and raise awareness of troublesome NPEs. They can share IP in a number of ways, including via licensing, cross-licensing, patent pools and patent clearing houses.

Drawing It All Together

The potential costs of patent infringement can be so severe that it would be unwise to ignore the issue of intellectual property during the course of designing your products. A company patent strategy can be invaluable because it defines a clear purpose for why your organisation may wish to protect its IP, in which territories around the world and for how long. This strategy can assist your patent attorney because they can operate and advise you with more clarity, having a clearer understanding of the scope of protection and approach that the organisation wishes to take.

Always assign responsibility to an individual within your design team to take ownership of any IP activities and coordinate with the patent attorney to ensure all necessary steps in the design creation process follow the company patent strategy. It's critically important that prior art searches are carried out as soon as a design concept has been finalised so that any potential infringement can be identified and necessary adjustments to the concept can be made. Unfortunately, leaving the searches to the end of the project, when investment costs have mounted up, could mean additional delays and costs and even the cancellation of the project.

32 CONTROL THE CREATIVE DIRECTION

'Every great design begins with an even better story.'

LORINDA MAMO

What Is the Rule?

What is creative direction? It is the theme or concept which unites a collection of products visually, in terms of their look and feel, covering elements such as colour, materials, finish, graphics and typography. As design leader, you can utilise creative direction as a tool to bring together all the visual touchpoints of your business and brand, from the product and packaging through to the advertising campaign, retail displays and online assets. This helps to raise brand awareness and loyalty as well as the perceived quality of your products, which will increase your market impact and sales.

The Problem

The meaning of creative direction isn't well understood by non-creatives, and there's often confusion about its value and how and when it should be implemented within the creative process and the wider business. Even among creatives, there is often misunderstanding around its exact definition. In fact, there isn't a definitive definition. The critical thing is that it should be agreed on and understood by everyone within the organisation so that there is a common language. The creative direction of a range of products can last for one collection, a season, a year, or longer if necessary, depending on the needs of the business.

Without creative direction, the message conveyed by products is often confusing for consumers. If the product looks and feels different to the packaging and marketing campaign, there is a dissonance that feels jarring – it's visually less appealing. If product ranges don't have visual harmony in their design and branding, they can't convey how they belong alongside one another. In this case, the business can easily lose out on cross-merchandising where, for example, consumers might purchase different fashion products with the same look and feel to create a complementary outfit. In both instances, product revenue takes a hit. The story of the creative direction should, therefore, seamlessly hold all elements of a design together for greater impact, awareness and visibility among shoppers and consumers. Without this cohesive narrative, the brand won't seem as culturally relevant and in line with current market trends to its target consumers – the audience it's trying to build a relationship with.

The Solution

Creative direction is best executed when led and approved by the single, uncompromised vision of the appointed design leader. The design leader

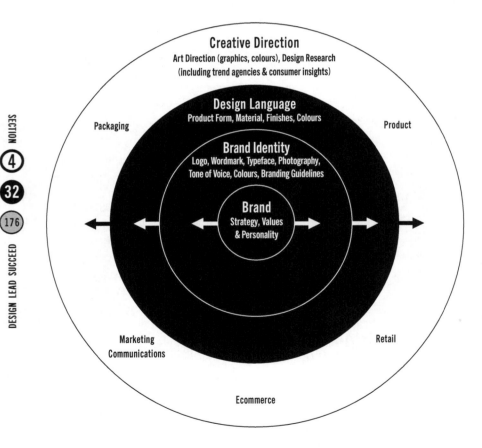

Figure 32.1 The creative direction's connection to the brand and business strategy

will be you if you hold the most senior design position within your organisation. The title 'creative director' is often given to this position in various industries, such as fashion. To help define the most coherent and pure interpretation of the creation direction, you should ideally have the authority of final approval over all visual assets across the business.

As we see in Figure 32.1, creative direction is another tool that helps the design team to fulfil the business strategy. The Adidas X Parley collaboration, which began in 2015, is a great example of where creative direction has been built to help deliver a strategic business objective. As I don't work for Adidas, I can only assume that they have a longer-term strategic business objective to make footwear and apparel products which are sustainable and 'help end plastic waste'. This helps to grow its market share with Gen Z consumers (born between 1997 and 2012) who, according to some research sources, care the most about the damage that manufacturing of consumer products is doing to the planet and environment. Collaborating with the charity Parley for the Oceans allows Adidas to partly fulfil its objective by associating itself with a cause which helps to reduce plastic waste and improves the health of the oceans. Adidas and Parley collaborated to create the first-ever running shoe made from upcycled plastic waste. The creative direction then formed a common visual thread which runs through the product to the marketing communications and retail unitary. The natural tone colour palette, using cream and emerald green, helps to communicate the story by conveying the feel of the ocean rather than artificial man-made industrial colour processes. The material used and thin wired texture of the exterior of the footwear also visually communicate the story as it has a resemblance to fishing net material, executed in a repeated wave effect which echoes the ocean's surface.

Consider the following aspects when building a creative direction:

The deductive approach – Sometimes called deductive reasoning, this is more of a top-down approach where the design leader uses their own research and intuition to define the creative direction theme or concept at the start. The design team then works on this theme to provide evidence that it works and that it's relevant to the consumer and the market. The advantage is that it can be quick if you're short on time.

The inductive approach – Also known as inductive reasoning, this is more of a bottom-up approach where the design team carries out research into the consumer, competitors, marketplace, materials, future trends etc. Then, through iterative reviewing and filtering of the research, distinct patterns emerge as potential creative direction themes. The advantage of this approach is that it's very democratic and empowers the team to autonomously discover the concept. The disadvantage is that it takes longer to compile the research and distil it down into a chosen creative direction.

Art direction – This is specifically the elements of the visual artwork, such as graphics and colour, within the creative direction. Once the designers know what the creative direction theme is all about, they can then use that as an anchor from which to build their colours and graphics to reinforce that theme.

Seasonal direction – Seasonal direction can be a variant or a minor evolution of the art direction (graphics) and the colour palette of a creative direction. It's often used to prolong a creative direction's relevance so it can be used across further product collections.

Stakeholder buy-in – Build a creative direction document which outlines the theme. It can be used to visually convey the overall idea and aesthetic of what a collection could look like when it's completed. This is of huge benefit because it allows stakeholders to review a concept and approve it before any costs are incurred.

Drawing It All Together

Creative direction is an invaluable storytelling design tool which supports the successful fulfilment of the business strategy. It can reinvigorate a brand each time it's used by maintaining its cultural relevance in the eyes of the consumer. It takes people on a journey, telling them the story of the product and the company, as well as their future vision.

33 ALWAYS HAVE A BACK-UP PLAN

'Never depend on those luck moments – they are gifts –
but instead always build your own back-up plan.'

BEAR GRYLLS

What Is the Rule?

The unexpected can occur on any design creation project at any time. The design creation process carries with it this constant and ever-present tension. There's an acknowledgement that changes to the design can occur due to limitations and restrictions in the manufacturing process or potential infringements of patents. This should be accepted because when you're trying to create anything new there's a level of experimentation and learning that's necessary. Very rarely does a concept design progress through to production and launch without a single alteration. This is especially true in complex products with multiple components that interact with one another.

The Problem

In the pursuit of technological advancement and innovation, you'll need to embrace uncertainty as you work within and beyond the limits of what is currently feasible to manufacture. Challenges can arise anywhere along the journey of design creation, from material properties and construction methods during production, through to durability issues when products are in market.

You need to be ready to react to common and imminent changes. You need to be flexible and agile. You need to be quick in your response with a clear, trialled-and-tested methodology for working through challenges and problems. Management guru Peter Drucker defined leadership as a 'foul weather' job. If you don't have a back-up plan and the tools and methodologies to navigate challenges, then you could fail as a leader.

The Solution

It's the things you don't see coming which hit you! And prevention is always better than a cure. So, efforts should be made to explore unforeseen risks before they become issues. I generally consider myself to be an optimist, but it's also beneficial to frequent the mindset of a pessimist so when unexpected issues arise, you are prepared to tackle them. It's better to be in a position where, if your original idea becomes untenable, there's an alternative concept to pursue.

Consider the following approaches to contingency planning:

Embed the contingency mindset – Take the opportunity to embed the mindset of contingency planning in all your team interactions. Challenge the team and ask the question, 'What is our back-up plan if this solution we've chosen doesn't work out?' Any key project decisions should be accompanied with back-up plans.

Minimise the downsides – Take out insurance policies. Don't overcommit on only one solution, because if problems arise, it'll take you longer to regroup and find an alternative. For example, select an alternative solution to develop in parallel with your chosen solution – perhaps one which is slightly easier to manufacture.

Utilise a versatile quality management design tool – The Ishikawa cause and effect diagram – or fishbone diagram as it is sometimes called – is a very accessible, intuitive and versatile quality management tool. The tool helps to explore and categorise any given situation and problem by separating the causes into the diagram branches of the 6 Ms: man, machine, material, maintenance, method and Mother Nature. From experience, this tool can be used to forecast problems at the beginning of a project, identify potential causes of a specific problem during a project or even to ideate possible solutions to explore as concept designs.

Utilise a comprehensive quality management design tool – Once a design concept has taken shape and developed into a chosen route with defined functionality, then a failure modes and effects analysis (FMEA) could be carried out to aid a smoother transition through to market launch. FMEA originally evolved in the aerospace and military industries, with use on highly complex projects such as NASA space missions. It helps to list all of the potential failures which could occur in a product, process or system. Then it analyses the effects and thus classifies the potential failures in order of importance based on severity, frequency and detection capacity. The tool's strength is in its rigour and capacity to bring all stakeholders on the project together to foresee and then act to mitigate problems. FMEA can be a big commitment to manage, and it may need a designated project lead. It's perhaps better suited to being applied in larger organisations which have the necessary resources or on key organisational projects which are critical for commercial success and survival.

Present a calm demeanour – When urgent issues arise on projects and time delays are critical, it's important to remain level-headed and calm as the leader to allow clear and logical thinking to permeate throughout the team. There'll be time after the event is resolved to dig deeper to understand where problems arose.

Drawing It All Together

Expect challenges and always think through to the end, or at least your next few steps, so that you can foresee alternative paths to follow if you experience problems. Plan but also recognise that the plan will change as soon as the next project activities begin. The challenges and consequent changes are part of the evolutionary journey of any design creation. In my opinion, as long as the design concept doesn't lose any of its differentiation and special essence, then the majority of the changes make the product better. The product will have evolved into a stronger solution from feedback and testing in order to better suit the user's reality. And by utilising quality management design tools, you'll always be prepared with a back-up plan whenever a risk becomes an issue.

SECTION

HOW TO ELEVATE THE DESIGN CREATION PROCESS

Why would you ever be satisfied with creating ordinary products? Surely the goal is to move from ordinary to extraordinary? To create extraordinary products which enrich the world and the lives and experiences of all those in it, you need to utilise methods of design creation which contribute to significant leaps in aesthetics and performance.

The rules in this section of the book will help you to dive into the process of elevating your design creation process:

DESIGN LEAD SUCCEED

34 CREATE A COMPELLING AND CONSISTENT DESIGN LANGUAGE

'Architecture as a language; if you are really good, you can be a poet.'

MIES VAN DER ROHE

What Is the Rule?

The products you create are silent ambassadors for your organisation's brand. Building a unique and desirable design language for your products will make a huge contribution to their success. As the design leader, you are responsible for creating, curating and guarding the design language across all touchpoints of the product and brand.

The Problem

Without a unique and desirable design language, your products will be harder for the consumer to identify in the marketplace and to build any sort of awareness and loyalty around. A design language will form design codes for how the team should treat each design element of form, finish, materials, colour and branding on products. Without these best practice guidelines, designers will generate solutions based on their own interpretation of style, thereby losing conformity and consistency across the product range. A compelling design language will allow your brand to stand out and be distinctive. For example, Christian Louboutin does this by utilising a very simple but highly visible and unforgettable signature detail on his shoes – a red-coloured sole. Even in the absence of a logo, the shoes can be quickly identified.

For a truly seamless brand experience, it is necessary for you as design leader to not only have control over the design language across the product range but also for every visual touchpoint for the consumer across the brand. This could include the appearance of the online presence, the in-store retail experience, the packaging etc. By having a single viewpoint and having an overview of the brand's aesthetic, you can execute a compelling and consistent consumer experience.

The Solution

Design language guidelines – or design codes – are a concise and powerful way to translate a brand's unique values and personality into tangible design elements such as form, materials, finish and colour. Of course, it is first necessary to have the brand's value and personality well-defined, which then helps to define the brand identity components such as logo, wordmark, typeface and tone of voice. These brand identity elements should work across the full breadth of mediums, both off and online.

Consider the following aspects in the implementation of your design language:

Set clear parameters for the design team – A design language provides the parameters for designers – both internal and external – to work within. This stops too much of their own personal style from overlaying the aesthetic of the product. It is a challenge to modify your personal design style to the handwriting of a brand, so the guidelines are an important tool to help keep the team (or external design consultants) on track and steer their input. Set clear instructions on how the brand identity, which includes elements such as the brand logo, should be applied to the product, packaging and point of sale unitary, perhaps influenced by its purpose and heritage, to provide them with guard rails.

Prioritise colour – Colour is one of the first things recognised by the human eye. You have only a few seconds with which to grab the attention of a shopper, so it is vital that the colour you choose is effective. How will consumers recognise your brand instinctively and instantly in a retail environment? Colour is your core tool. Think about how it can be best used across all elements, including on the product, packaging, branding and in communications.

Coherence within product ranges – Does the range of products look like it belongs to the same family even without the brand logo applied? This is a good test of the strength and quality of the design language guidelines. It should be an aesthetic language of visual identity which flows across categories and ranges. But bear in mind that the key here is 'consistency' of execution. This approach must be repeated many times across products for it to become visually ingrained in the culture and environment of your consumer.

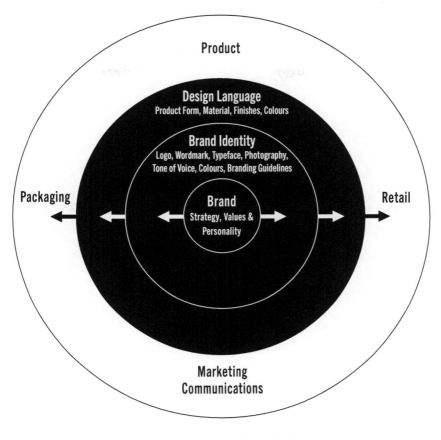

Figure 34.1 The creation of a design language

Drawing It All Together

Building a compelling and consistent design language accelerates the growth of brand equity. Figure 34.1 above shows the position of 'design language' guidelines in relation to brand values, personality and identity. It's only once these elements have been clearly defined that the design language can be layered on top. But crucially, design language is the visual vehicle through which the brand can be communicated to the user through the execution of form, materials, colour and finish.

35 UNDERSTAND WHAT THE CONSUMER VALUES MOST

'Research amongst consumers. Find out how they think about your kind of product, what language they use when they discuss the subject, what attributes are important to them, and what promise would be most likely to make them buy your brand.'

DAVID OGILVY

What Is the Rule?

Unlocking the emotional desires of consumers is the key to designing successful products. They must fulfil a need. But what is it that leads to products becoming truly loved and, ultimately, highly profitable? We must uncover the hidden code in the marketplace – the hierarchy of consumers' most valued needs – to guide the design of our products. Test and validate, according to those needs, at every step of the design creation process to ensure they are being fulfilled.

The Problem

Products are predominantly used as enablers to improve our experience of the world based on what we most desire and need.

Thus, when designing any product, particularly in a new area, it is critical to define and understand the group of people you are designing for. Once you know who your targets are, it's then necessary to begin building a list of their needs. You may have an exhaustive list, but if you don't know which needs are most important to them, you risk placing your energy and focus in the wrong areas to the detriment of the final design. You can also misstep by failing to understand the variety of different user groups who may have very different needs in relation to the same product. And designing a product shouldn't end with understanding the needs and desires of only the user. It's also advisable to investigate and predict the product's impact on the environment it's used in and the bystanders it may interact with. Google Glass was an example of a cutting-edge technology which offered a groundbreaking user experience, but the use of the glasses became less acceptable because of the environment it operated in – public spaces. It threw up issues of privacy, ethics and social norms that hadn't been encountered before. The use of the product became more and more restricted over time because of these concerns. The fact that the technology was placed on your face also made it extremely difficult to ascertain if recording was taking place or not.

The Solution

Highly successful products meet the most important user needs by delivering outstanding and unmatched functional performance. By understanding these needs, and their order of importance, you can create a vital connection between them and your product. This hidden code locked within your customer's hierarchy of needs will help you to tap into their values and desires – the essence of why people buy.

However, it's worth noting that function isn't the only consideration when it comes to what consumers want. The aesthetics of a product are often incredibly important to people, and because it taps into an emotional 'want', it can sometimes override all other needs in the purchase decision-making process. However, it's always difficult to test the consumer's preference between form and function because they are intrinsically linked within any physical object.

Consider these three methods of user-centred research that will help you to discover the consumer's hierarchy of needs: observation, interviews and surveys:

Observation – Observation, which is also termed 'ethnography', helps in the early stages with identifying needs. People cannot always articulate what they need most, so watching rather than asking can be a better way to understand what's really going on. Sometimes, when trying to improve an existing product, a breakthrough comes from observing the current product in use or from the designer using the product for themselves and rationally breaking down the experience. This process often allows the unmet need for the consumer to surface. You might see how current products do not fully cater for their needs or how steps in the process could be removed to reduce the time required to use them. Alternatively, you might see how an additional feature can be introduced to the product to increase safety or reduce the consumer's stress levels. If you are considering an entirely new invention with a purpose that fulfils an unmet need, it might be useful to observe what people use instead of this new product or how they get around this unmet need.

Interviews – Arrange interviews with individuals, pairs or groups of your chosen consumer. It's good to do this in their natural environment so they are more relaxed and honest. Use open questioning techniques, avoiding yes and no answers, to allow the interviewee to elaborate and describe their experiences in their own words. It's useful to ask a group to bring in their current products as this prompts discussion. Various methods for coding and analysing the results can then be used to try and tease out trends and themes for further testing as well as a draft needs hierarchy.

Surveys – Based on the results of the coding from the interviews, you can then create and share a survey to a much larger number of target users. This allows you to test your needs hierarchy by asking the participants to rank their needs in relation to the product in order of importance. The more responses you receive, the more confident you can be that your results represent the average of the target user group.

Once your hierarchy of needs are defined, they serve as excellent guiding parameters for your team. They will help you pinpoint which performance improvement will be most critical and appreciated by the consumer and thus help you to decide where to direct your designers' energy.

The design team should also provide the list of prioritised user needs to the marketing function in the research stage of the project, before the product is even designed, so that they can start building their potential marketing claims which will feature on campaign communications, packaging and retail unitary.

Drawing It All Together

Users are driven to buy because of their needs and desires. If you can tap into what they most value, you can design a product that will thrive in the marketplace. Prioritise user-centred research to discover their hierarchy of needs, and this will give you a clear set of guiding parameters in your design creation process. These are the factors which will drive their purchasing decisions.

36 CONSULT WITH THE CONSUMER DURING DESIGN

'The role of the architect or the designer is that of a very good, thoughtful host, all of whose energy goes into trying to anticipate the needs of his guests.'

CHARLES EAMES

What Is the Rule?

Building large testing groups of your target consumers will effectively allow you to co-create the product with them, dramatically increasing the probability of success when your product launches. These user groups test and offer feedback on your design concepts throughout the creation process, helping to nudge you in the right direction as you iterate and improve on ideas. This will help to build confidence in your approach, and it will support your decision-making as you navigate your way towards a final solution.

The Problem

It's essential to gauge whether your new product will sell successfully. Having a better measure of this throughout the creation process will help you steer the project more effectively. Your intuition, accumulated from years of experience in the category area of your product, will help you to understand with a certain level of confidence what works and what doesn't for the target consumer. But you need a tool which replicates the actual reaction and response that will occur when your consumer experiences the product in the market. Imagine how useful a tool this would be to filter and review your ideas.

The Solution

Find and recruit at least one user group for your project who can help to consult on the product through the design creation process. Working with the users will help build insight as you progress. Here are the key considerations when building and working with the user group:

Find the right users – Assess and filter your user group to ensure that they are a typical representation of your chosen consumer in terms of demographics and behaviours.

Protect your IP – You need to protect your intellectual property: it is important to use participants who agree to sign a non-disclosure agreement (NDA). This means that they agree not to share any confidential details of your project until it is launched to market. This approach is not fully watertight, but it will help to protect your idea and allow you to seek and file patent protection when the time is right. (*Please note that it is always highly recommended to seek the advice of an intellectual property attorney whenever considering aspects of protecting your ideas*).

Agree the rules of engagement – Make sure they are aware of how the process will work from the start, which might include how you compensate them for their time. But beware, the most honest feedback can often result when participants are not paid. Paying them may skew their reactions. You could consider offering them a gift of a free version of the product, when and if it is launched, so they have a vested interest in trying to make the product as good as it can be.

Use multiple user groups – If you have the time and available resources, you can benefit from even greater confidence levels in your testing if you have multiple user groups from different geographical locations. This approach helps to triangulate your results. In past projects, I even involved different user groups at different stages of the design creation process. There were groups I used from start to finish who were able to chart how the product evolved for them, and groups that I used only towards the end whose experience had not been tarnished by unreliable early prototypes.

Consider how to ask questions – A critical part is 'how' you ask the questions as well as 'who' you ask and 'when' and 'where' you ask them. There is a whole discipline of market research that will offer guidance on how best to extract and analyse feedback. Beware of the alpha personality. Their opinion can override others and echo through the test session. Try to interview participants separately at certain points so that each individual's opinions can be fed back accurately and honestly. When dominant figures give their opinions, the majority may follow or be less inclined to disagree with their viewpoint.

Don't ignore negative feedback – Often, the listening may be difficult to handle when the feedback is brutal in response to early concepts and prototypes, but it is important to react, make changes accordingly and retest. This is the whole point. You need to listen and learn from the user group. You will probably have more tough days of poor responses in the earlier stages of the project than good days, and that's fine. You will improve. Never ignore negative feedback because it can be invaluable.

Drawing It All Together

By utilising a user group as part of your design creation process, you will have dramatically de-risked your project. There will be a much higher probability of success if you already know how users feel about it and whether their needs and concerns have been integrated into the design.

37 HARNESS THE POWER OF LITERATURE REVIEWS

'If I have seen further it is by standing on the shoulders of giants.'

ISAAC NEWTON

What Is the Rule?

How can we possibly know everything ourselves? Even the most intuitive designer needs an understanding of the most up-to-date theories and technologies that apply to their design creation challenge. It is only then that they are equipped to produce something that moves the industry forward by building on the progress made by others. But where can we find this information? In literature reviews.

The Problem

To achieve the greatest outcome, it's in our interests to find out what has gone before so that we can iterate and improve on it. It's a waste of our precious time and resources to learn purely from our own experiences and mistakes when we are walking a path that has already been trodden. We need to acquire the knowledge and skills of the pioneers in our particular area of design. There is a wealth of information out there that can inform our ideas and design solutions if we look for it. But when a project begins, we don't have unlimited scope to do endless research. We need a method of rapidly building our knowledge in our area of specialisation in the minimum time possible.

Solution

Much of the knowledge you seek is held within academic research journals. These document the process, testing and findings of theories in the quest to expand our knowledge in a particular field. Work like this is going on every day around the world, driven by educational institutions. And these findings are published for the greater good.

You can explore the relevant academic research when a new design project begins in a 'literature review'. However, a literature review can go far beyond journals. It covers all previously published work that is relevant to your product, from government publications to conference reports to books and newspapers. It's absolutely essential to build this into the research phase of the design creation process once you are clear on the design challenge and have your design brief.

Consider these suggestions when developing a policy on literature reviews:

Remind your team how important a literature review is – Do this by reinforcing how the process of researching the existing literature on a topic area allows gaps in their knowledge to be identified and, even more importantly, how it helps to confirm if the team's research findings are original and not evident in past literature.

Utilise reviews of the research – A useful shortcut to reviewing the recent research in an area is to look for articles which have already done this for you. Often called a 'literature review' or a 'review of the literature', the authors will collate the most relevant studies and provide their own summary of the findings. If nothing else, this is a great starting point for your own further study of these theories.

Find a local university and build links – This relationship will help you to prioritise research in your design creation process. They may help with access to the research papers you require. Or you may be able to receive research assistance for funding a postgraduate student to build the literature review using your key search words.

Spend wisely on the most relevant journal subscriptions – There's a caveat with journals: a great deal of the knowledge you require is not freely available. It's generated or provided by commercial organisations which, quite rightly, protect their intellectual capital for future competitive advantage. Look carefully for the most relevant sources of information in your field when choosing a journal subscription.

Capitalise on open access research – There's a substantial amount of academic literature which is freely available to read. Suggested databases are listed in the further reading section of this book.

Find research field experts – Every academic journal represents a doorway to a subject matter expert. Your research will focus on specific areas of knowledge in the quest to deliver your objectives, and the most cited and prevalent authors in the most relevant literature will highlight potential project partners. Chapter 40, *Engage with Technical Experts,* discusses this topic in more detail.

Upskill designers in their research methods – It's worthwhile helping designers to become adept in research methods because, beyond improving the quality of the research and insights generated, it will aid in strengthening their analytical thinking on any project. If your team is of a sufficient size, you may also consider creating a research manager role with responsibility for leading and managing the collation of insights at the front end of projects (which will include the generation of literature reviews).

If you embed this process into your design projects, you'll begin armed with an embarrassment of riches in terms of insights. You'll be standing on the shoulders of giants, at a much higher vantage point, with greater clarity over your project and which course to chart. Your next challenge is what to do with these insights. Hopefully, you'll be able to translate them into tangible and credible functional benefits that will increase the performance of your product.

Drawing It All Together

Carrying out a literature review at the beginning of a project will ensure that you have the very best foundation to begin your design creation process. This method of acquiring insights and knowledge should be considered a prerequisite to any project. Without new insights, the project may struggle to produce a step change in performance.

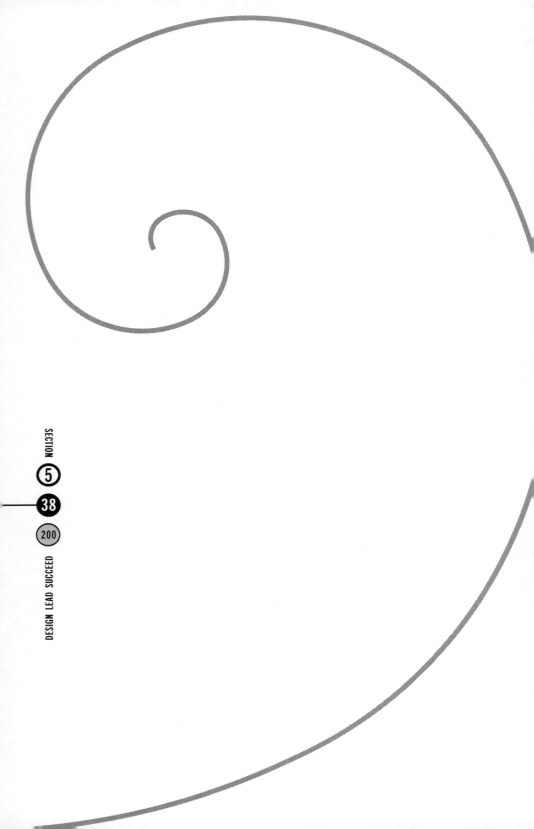

DESIGN LEAD SUCCEED

38 PUT MATERIALS FRONT AND CENTRE

'No design is possible until the materials with which you design are completely understood.'

MIES VAN DER ROHE

What Is the Rule?

Materials are pivotal enablers in design. New materials enable paradigm shifts in product performance. Give materials the prominence they deserve in your decision-making and reimagine how they can contribute to the design creation process. Shift resources so that material sourcing and development can be at the heart of your team's work. They should be prioritised from the very beginning to the end of the product journey and considered in every design decision.

The Problem

Materials are almost more influential than any other component or consideration in the design of a product. They can make or break its success. The multinational chemical company Dupont developed an imitation leather material called Corfam. Introduced in 1963, it was first utilised in shoes because of its supposed improved durability and easy-to-clean high-gloss finish compared to natural leather. But unfortunately, consumers noticed the disadvantages of the material – its increased stiffness and lack of breathability – which possibly contributed to the product being withdrawn from the market in 1971.

In recent years, the stakes have been raised again by the government-driven urgency to save our oceans and natural habitats and the species which live within them from man-made waste. It's not just important but a necessity to use materials which are from sustainable sources, can be recycled or are part of a circular manufacturing process. You have a choice to either damage or heal the planet for future generations with your selection of materials.

The Solution

Prioritise materials selection and specification, giving it your respect and focus. While I was working as part of a team tasked with redesigning an aircraft interior, the decision was made to change components in the aircraft passenger seats to carbon fibre. This material selection allowed fire retardancy regulations to be met, but it also meant the weight and size of the seat could be decreased, which allowed for fuel cost savings from weight reduction and also slightly increased leg room between seats for an improved consumer experience. Consider the following steps when integrating materials development and decision-making into the core of your design creation process:

Hire expertise in materials – Find someone who truly understands materials science and product design and recruit them to your team. Do not rely solely on the recommendations and knowledge of your factory or the manufacturer's technical team. You need someone who can look at materials from a design perspective and focus on this as their priority.

Improve team knowledge and awareness – Set up materials training and develop the knowledge of your designers. This is essential learning for their craft and it will act to inspire them. Develop a common technical language among the team for the parameters specifying the materials.

Continuously research – Regularly scout for new materials and inspiration. This should be the key focus of your expert in materials, but it should also be something your designers get involved in.

Set up a materials library – Create a research and development materials resource in parallel with the design creation process so that new materials can be tried, tested and validated for manufacture well in advance of being specified in a new design project. The risks and implications of using materials without enough testing can be damaging to a brand's reputation and the financial position of the organisation.

Consider how materials can combine – Think about if and how you can combine materials. Test your ideas to confirm they are compatible. Can the materials be fixed together or bonded in the manufacturing process without failure? In what order do the materials need to be bonded together for maximum strength and durability?

Standard or bespoke? – Consider whether you should use off-the-shelf materials or bespoke materials, which can be fabrics or polymers that are created specifically for your product or range of products. Standard materials are often more widely available and easy to source, as well as cheaper than bespoke materials. However, the material solutions you develop are exclusive to your brand, which helps to protect your competitive advantage in the marketplace. Indeed, if you're able to get patent protection for a new and innovative material you've developed, which proves important to the industry, this could give you huge financial returns.

Drawing It All Together

Your choice of materials has a huge impact on the success of your design, and so it should be prioritised by you as leader and by your team. The use of new materials may allow new functionalities and performance levels to be achieved, and this opens up opportunities, whether that's selling more products, increasing the level of customer satisfaction, boosting the reputation of the brand or producing something truly innovative that could impact society positively.

39 WEAR YOUR OWN PRODUCTS!

'Eat your own dog food.'

DAVID CUTLER

What Is the Rule?

Encourage your team to immerse themselves in the environment of your products and the people who use and wear them. They must experience them for themselves so they can understand the user's journey, what works and what doesn't. This will ultimately allow them to make more informed decisions as designers. As the design leader, you absolutely must wear and test the products yourself in order to lead by example and inspire your team. The goal is to create the very best products in the world!

The Problem

If designers create products based solely on feedback from other people, even if those people are the target consumers, then they are carrying around a large personal 'blind spot' and missing a great opportunity for deeper insight and learning. Without experiencing the product firsthand, they cannot compare responses from testing feedback to what they have felt themselves. It is much harder for them, in these circumstances, to distinguish the 'noise', or random comments, from the actual truth of what is going on between the product and the user. Lacking a user's perspective, the designer's understanding of the problem they are solving is incomplete, and this introduces risk into the design process.

The Solution

There is no better way to build empathy with the people you are designing for and gain a greater understanding of the problems they face than by immersing yourself in their world and wearing the products you've created for them.

By adding your own experiences to the feedback you gain from user testing, computer-simulated testing and laboratory-condition testing, you can triangulate results, which will increase your confidence levels and clarity over decisions. You'll also become much more confident in presenting the ideas because you'll be able to use the language of the tribe as well as personal examples of how the product performs; this holds much more power for an audience.

Consider the following ideas for incorporating greater use of your products into your daily routine:

Encourage your team to wear the products – You could make it a core principle of your design team to wear the products and encourage them by helping to remove the barriers to this activity. For example, give them an open invitation to use working hours for these wear tests, providing transportation and access to a test environment if necessary.

Test prototypes – Don't just test the products that have been released. Test the product prototypes from the early research stages of any design project so that you can see what's working and what's not. In this way, you can immerse yourself in the user experience.

Join the tribe – Get involved in the activity the products are used for and learn the techniques and skills. If you are designing outdoor equipment, you should get out on the trails and immerse yourself in hiking and camping. Make it a hobby if you enjoy the activity enough. It is your responsibility to know the technical product details inside out and to integrate yourself into the community of these users. You will become trusted and build a highly valuable network. I successfully swam the English Channel as part of a relay team in 2019. It was an amazing personal journey, but I also learnt invaluable insights about the products and users that would have been impossible to acquire from merely asking questions from the sidelines.

Test competitor products – Test and wear your competitors' products to understand how your creation differs. By feeling the benefits yourself and how they compare to your designs, rather than only seeing and hearing what other people are saying, you'll experience much more acute insights.

Drawing It All Together

In becoming a product tester, you'll produce a better thought-through solution to the problem. It will help you to refine your designs as you'll understand the nuances of the user journey. There can obviously be constraints to wearing or testing your own products, if you are designing an interior for a first-class aircraft seat, for example. But still, if the very best insights and design solutions are to arise, the designer should ideally be given access to the product and the opportunity to live the user's experience.

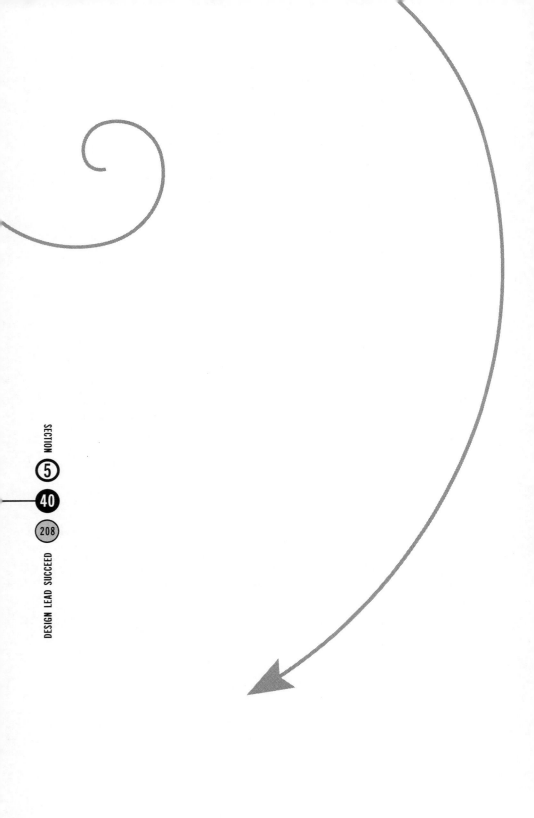

40 ENGAGE WITH TECHNICAL EXPERTS

'When two or more people co-ordinate in a spirit of harmony, and work towards a definite objective, they place themselves in position, through that alliance, to absorb power directly from the great universal storehouse of Infinite Intelligence.'

NAPOLEON HILL

What Is the Rule?

Fresh insights can create breakthroughs in product innovation. So, remember to engage with technical experts from different fields of study and acquire specialised expertise and knowledge faster than your competitors in order to boost your product success rate.

The Problem

If your design team is challenged with finding novel solutions to an already exhausted product area – perhaps one which has been covered by your team multiple times or one which is completely new and unknown – then fresh ideas and approaches may be required. Generating genuinely original product inventions can require specific technical knowledge and skills in particular areas of research. This can help to fuel new insights and ways of approaching problems. However, acquiring these within your existing team can take valuable time, learning and practice. Time is always a scarce resource and the process of creation must be accelerated if you are to compete in the marketplace and break away from the status quo.

The Solution

Jumpstart your design creation process with an injection of inspiration and specialist knowledge and skills by engaging with technical experts. They will have already built up and acquired the key knowledge and skills which you need to discover new angles and make breakthroughs in your project. You never know what golden nuggets they can offer you.

I personally benefitted from this approach when discussing a design problem around swimming goggles with an academic expert in optometry. I was struggling to find a solution which would help to make goggles faster through the water by reducing drag, but not at the expense of clear vision. We discussed the science of optometry and how vision is altered when looking through a lens underwater. His insights made my colleague and me consider the design problem from a different perspective. Following that conversation, I experienced an epiphany in my way of thinking, which resulted in me proposing a new lens shape profile. At that time, the majority of racing swimming goggles incorporated a flat, elliptical lens. My colleagues and I developed a flat lens shape which also had a vertical plane bend in the surface, allowing the lens to continue to wrap around the surface of the face with a single curvature. This was in contrast to the double curvature shape mostly seen in the market which creates distortion underwater. Our lens shape also reduced the required size of the goggle, which meant drag was reduced and speed could increase through the water.

Consider the following steps when searching for and engaging with technical experts:

Finding your expert – Once your area of research has been identified, search for your experts in relevant industries and academic research. They may be published authors on the topic, article columnists or they may have had peer-reviewed research published. Often, it is good to search your own network of business contacts and ask for ideas and recommendations of relevant individuals as they might be more likely to speak to you as an act of goodwill. Social media channels and platforms such as LinkedIn are also excellent resources for finding experts as you can find out who has currency on particular topics and what they have produced on the subject.

Building a relationship – Once you have found your expert, discuss and agree on the remit of your conversation. Share your story and project challenges with them. Often, they'll be happy to share their expert opinion and insight if they see the relationship as mutually beneficial. Depending on the stage of your project, you may need to request that the conversation be covered by a non-disclosure agreement (NDA) so that the details cannot be shared with any external parties (it is always best to take legal advice when setting up an appropriate NDA). Meeting the expert in their own working environment is often fascinating for you and easier for them. The conversation may be better too as they will be more relaxed and at home in their own domain.

Alternatives to building a relationship – A conversation with an expert is not always necessary. Sometimes a visit to a conference or listening to a speech by an expert may be enough to inspire a change of thinking and approach to a problem. This also requires less effort as you don't need to convince them to allocate time for you.

Using groups of experts – Deepen the impact on your project by bringing a number of experts together in an arranged group workshop with the purpose of discussing and debating your area of research. This approach can be arranged using the Chatham House Rule, where all attendees agree not to disclose what is discussed but each can benefit personally from insights in the session.

Developing a long-term relationship – Some connections with experts may develop into strong working relationships with their services being paid for when needed. As you've already spent valuable time finding the right person, this might save you resources in the long-run and encourage more productive feedback if they are invested in the relationship.

Drawing It All Together

Utilising external technical experts to boost your breadth of knowledge and skills could dramatically increase your chances of success in creating novel solutions and staying ahead of the curve. It will also mean that you have great foresight in terms of future industry movements, something that could pay off for years to come in terms of your competitive advantage. So, crack on and find those experts.

41 DON'T LOSE THE ART OF SKETCHING

'Drawing keeps one fit like physical exercises, perhaps acts like water to a plant and it lessens the danger of repeating oneself and getting into a formula.'

HENRY MOORE

What Is the Rule?

The pen is a key for unlocking ideas hidden in the mind. As a designer, sketching is an essential part of your craft; as a leader, it will help you to communicate ideas and suggestions for design changes while building mutual respect and connection with your team. This is a skill you should also encourage your design team to practice regularly so they don't lose the art of expressing their ideas by hand.

The Problem

There comes a point when your ideas cannot adequately be conveyed verbally with your team, as their theoretical nature means they are harder to grasp and less inspiring. This is particularly true in a creative and design context where people think and process visually. Sketching by hand can be the quickest and most direct route to turning an intangible thought into a tangible idea that can be shared. Larger, more complex projects require more designers working together, and so clear communication is critical. Sketching becomes even more important when considering the greater challenge of working with colleagues and collaborators in different parts of the world where English is not their first language; it's a common language. As leaders, however, with a much broader remit than design, we may find that our sketching skills fall into disrepair.

The Solution

When leading a project, a simple sketch can clearly articulate a point of view or proposed change much more effectively than a verbal suggestion. With this in mind, try not to lose your sketching skills as a leader and include them in your process as often as possible.

I love to sketch. As a child, I spent countless hours drawing what I saw in the world and copying nature. Then my drawings evolved to visualising my idea of the future, which led me to enter and win a Nissan car design of the future competition when I was 10 years old. This inspired me to keep drawing and ultimately led me to study automotive design at university and pursue a career in design.

The more frequently you draw, the more fluidly the ideas will flow through your mind, to your pen and onto paper. And the more you practice, the more accomplished you become at sketching. Consider these ways of incorporating sketching into your routine and design leadership activities:

• Carry a small sketchbook and pen around with you in your pocket so that when inspiration hits, you're able to capitalise on your rush of creativity. When I was a young designer working in London, I would often scribble ideas and designs down when they popped into my head while travelling on the train to work.

• Encourage sketching in every project by making it a part of the creation process. This is where you, as design leader, can help to inspire others as to the value of sketch work by using it in your steering of design reviews and informal chats regarding design work. You can do this using your own sketched suggestions of alternative ideas or surfacing details, for example.

• Create a set of common underlay guidance templates for projects. These can be used under the pages of sketch pads by all designers so that there is consistency in scale and proportion when they sketch. This will help in reviewing, comparing and evaluating ideas in design reviews.

• Sketching isn't just for design ideas. Use a sketched diagram in meetings with non-designers to help them visualise a complex topic of discussion for greater clarity and better decision-making.

• Accept that sketching has its limits and isn't a natural process for everyone. When creating 3D objects, there comes a point when 2D sketching isn't enough and it's necessary to move towards a physical prototype and a 3D CAD representation. Some people also prefer to sculpt their ideas in 3D using various media – whether it's foam, wood or clay. Depending on the type of product being designed, sketching may also take a different form. For example, apparel designers may sketch style lines on fabric on a mannequin.

Drawing It All Together

Whether as a design leader or designer, the art of sketching can greatly enhance the process of generating ideas and working through functional and aesthetic problems. Once the skill has been learnt, it cannot be lost, but like riding a bike, it needs to be practised regularly to improve your proficiency and the quality of results. Critically, sketching should be seen as a global language among artists, designers and engineers, and so it's value as a method of communication cannot be overstated.

42 MAKE HERO FEATURES VISIBLE ON PRODUCTS

'The keyword of our profession is "desire".
You have to create a desire.'

KARL LAGERFELD

What Is the Rule?

To compete in a saturated marketplace, you need to find a way to stand out from the crowd. Your design might have unique and special features that set it apart from other similar products on the market, but if these are invisible to the consumer, it's much harder to grab their attention and make it commercially successful. Marketing and sales can help to convey these unique selling points (USPs) via their communication tools, packaging or point of sale unitary, but they can only do so much. By designing products in a way that clearly highlights their 'hero' features, you can help to drive consumer interest and the desire to purchase.

The Problem

The choice of available products for consumers continues to grow year on year as brands react ever more quickly to changing trends and consumer behaviour. You might have designed a product which offers a unique and improved solution to a consumer need, but it can go unnoticed if the 'hero' features which achieve this are hidden in the design. Unfortunately, lots of design teams fail to make the tangible benefits visible in their product's aesthetics during the creation process, but doing so can boost market awareness.

The Solution

Many of the most successful sports products have been created by brands that understand how to visually highlight their defining features. They have designed the product in a way which allows the functional technologies that are most desirable to the consumer to be seamlessly integrated into the aesthetics and, therefore, made visible. Sayan Chatterjee proposed the visible-invisible rule to aid designers in their decision-making process as to what technologies to make visible and which to hide. If the consumer doesn't care about a technology, it can be hidden or re-engineered to reduce costs. If they do care about a technology – i.e. it's a 'hero' feature – then you should make it visible to them in the design, even if it increases costs, in order to differentiate yourself from the competition. Figure 42.1 outlines this visible-invisible rule.

I could easily apply this rule in the context of my own work designing sportswear and sports performance equipment. We prioritise the needs of athletes and consumers – and therefore what features they care about –

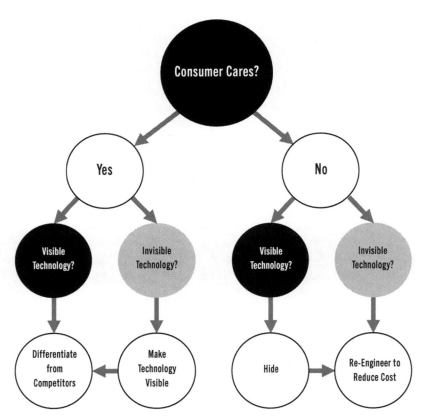

Figure 42.1 – Applying the visible-invisible rule

by undertaking design research via interviews, focus groups, surveys and direct observation. It's very often the case for performance sports products that our users want 'form to follow function', and so a new functional part of the product usually takes centre stage. The aesthetic or design language then follows from this and is sympathetic to this feature. In a previous job, I was responsible for designing the interior cab of a train where the driver sat. Driving a train is a complex task with multiple procedures for the driver to execute to ensure the safety of the vehicle and the passengers. To help make the driver's experience as simple as possible, and incur minimum fatigue, it was necessary to design the layout of the controls in a way which considered the sightlines and positions of controls deemed primary and secondary operations. Primary control operations were the most important needs of the driver, so these were brought within the closest ergonomic proximity of the driver's sightlines and limbs. And to make these primary controls more visible, they were coloured differently – usually red, to contrast against the secondary controls – and placed on halo-shaped, darkly-coloured panels to further enhance the speed of recognition by the driver.

In my opinion, one of the greatest executions of this visible-invisible rule being applied successfully is the Nike Air Max running shoe. Back in 1978, Nike introduced air cushioning technology into the midsoles of their running shoes. However, it wasn't until 1987, while designing the Nike Air Max, that the renowned Nike footwear designer Tinker Hatfield made the air cushion visible and part of the external aesthetic of the shoe. We all now know that it appears as an air bubble in the midsole. Apparently, Tinker Hatfield was inspired by the architecture of the Centre Pompidou in Paris, where the inner workings of the building are externally visible and an integral part of the overall design. In doing so, he revolutionised the footwear market forever and created an iconic design feature. Running consumers desired comfortable, well-fitting and lightweight running shoes, and the visible air bubble on the Nike Air Max visually communicated these attributes while differentiating itself from competitor brands.

Drawing It All Together

Always keep the visible-invisible rule in mind when you design your product. Consider what your target consumer needs and desires most and how the features of your product fulfil those needs. If these 'hero' features are hidden, you are missing a huge opportunity to grab the attention of your audience and make them aware of those USPs. With a little thought, you can market your product through your design language and help to make it commercially successful.

43 BE FAMILIAR AND UNIQUE

'We had to be right on trend, not too far ahead or too far behind. And we had to hit the bull's-eye every single time.'

TOMMY HILFIGER

What Is the Rule?

What is the key to commercial success and widespread adoption when designing a product? There are lots of contributing factors at play, but there is one magic ratio that you need to master. Your product must be familiar and yet unique to the consumer. It's a fine balance that a designer must judge in order to unlock consumer interest and propel them towards choosing your brand above others. If the product isn't familiar enough, with comparable features to its competitors, then it could be discounted by the consumer as irrelevant before the final purchasing decision is made. But once it manages to pass this test, the product also needs to be unique enough to differentiate itself from competitors and thus stand out as the most appealing choice.

There are exceptions to this rule. Global superbrands, such as Coca-Cola, are already trusted market leaders who are recognised by the consumers in their category, so they'll automatically receive purchasing consideration if they are within an accessible cost range. However, most brands will need to be more savvy in the way they design and present their products in order to be heard above the noise of the marketplace.

The Problem

For products to gain traction, attain critical mass and then achieve mass market adoption and the commercial success that comes with it, there needs to be enough consumers willing to purchase the product and then repeat their purchase in an ever-expanding virtuous circle.

But at the point of purchase, in the brick-and-mortar store or online, how can the product attract the consumer for long enough that they decide to buy? Without a clear point of differentiation, the product will be competing against other competitors on considerations such as price, brand loyalty and style. Market-leading brands have greater advantages over smaller and newer entrants to the category in these situations because there is already a certain level of brand awareness in the mind of the consumer. It is essential, therefore, that your product provides unique qualities that are compelling to the consumer and which allow it to stand out in the marketplace. But winning the consumer over is not quite as simple as that!

Daniel Kahneman and Amos Tversky articulated the nuances of the consumer's dilemma in making the correct decision when purchasing products in their research into behavioural economics. Their 'loss aversion' theory explains how we perceive products as providing a risk of both loss and a chance for gain based on how much uniqueness they possess. There is a propensity for losses to be felt more strongly than the pleasure of gains. And so, there may be a limit to how much uniqueness will be accepted by the consumer. There needs to be a level of familiarity and recognition in terms of the product features and design to reassure them of its benefits. Obviously, all consumers are different, but considering the population as a whole, there will be a majority that are cautious in their choices. A balance must therefore be found; your product must be both familiar and unique, as outlined in Figure 43.1.

The Solution

The solution is to design any given product in a way which balances the necessary level of familiarity, so as to reassure the consumer, with a level of uniqueness that the consumer finds desirable and eye-catching.

Consider the following approaches to making a product familiar enough for the consumer:

Consumer journey mapping – This helps to highlight current user behaviour and rituals when using a product, which can help to define some of the most familiar aspects of the design. This is similar to an ergonomic task analysis of the consumer's interaction with the product during its operation. It's a useful exercise as it helps to break down the functioning of the product's separate parts, which can then be considered, designed and improved in isolation before putting them back together or removing them from the process altogether to make the functioning even simpler.

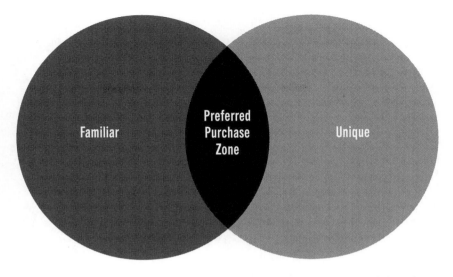

Figure 43.1 – Targeting the consumer sweet spot between the familiar and the unique

Comparable features – Does your product possess all of the key features and benefits of the main competitor products? Key features should address the various core needs and desires of the consumer which solve their pain points. Byron Sharp, in his book *How Brands Grow*, suggests that for branded products to remain part of the consumer selection process in retail, they must ensure there isn't a reason 'not to buy'. So, match competitors on product specification and ensure there aren't any negative aspects which give consumers a reason to dismiss the product, such as harmful manufacturing processes or materials.

Consider the following approaches to making the product unique enough for the consumer:

Unique selling points (USPs) – Try to create unique features which are relevant and highly valued by the consumer you are targeting. Aerodynamic cycling equipment, for example, is highly desirable to time trial cyclists and triathletes because the shape and surface texture of the products can help to reduce drag forces from air flow, which then increases rider speed and improves overall race performance. Test your USPs through design research and development. The USPs will resonate strongly with the consumer if they can be backed by supporting claims with data showing a significant percentage improvement to prove the benefits. You could be unique in the product or unique in the production process. The effect on the consumer will be even greater if the claimed improvements are easy to see in the product itself – for example, an outdoor backpack that is actually more comfortable to wear and lighter – and their expectations of the product are exceeded!

Competitive advantage – If the USP features are derived from a particular manufacturing process that is unknown to the competition or the functional design of the product is novel with patent protection in the regions of the world where you manufacture and sell into the biggest markets, then you'll benefit from prolonged competitive advantage. The feature could be part of the secret recipe. In product terms, this might be the material/fabric specification which provides specific properties.

Storytelling – A strong and engaging story behind the design of any product helps to capture the imagination of the consumer. It also explains and justifies its unique features so that the purchase decision doesn't feel as much of a risk.

Everett Rogers, in his book *Diffusion of Innovations,* built on this idea of balancing the familiar and the unique. He added a layer of secondary factors that he felt contributed to how quickly a product innovation would be successfully adopted by the consumer. These include the factors of 'relative advantage' (the level to which the new product innovation is perceived to be an improvement over its predecessors), 'compatibility' (how well the new product innovation is perceived in line with the current values, social norms and behaviours of the consumer), 'complexity' (how well the product innovation can be understood and operated), 'trialability' (the ability of the product innovation to be available for the consumer to test and trial on a limited basis to help them perceive the benefits), and 'observability' (how much more readily the consumers will adopt the new product innovation if they see evidence of it being used by others and it working well).

There's also a caveat to this rule of being both familiar and unique. Where a product includes new technology and is a true step change in the world, it needs to be more unique because the function, by its very nature, is radically different. Maybe it removes many steps from the previous consumer process, or it's a new solution entirely. Regardless, to ensure the product is intuitive to use, there should still be consideration as to what consumers currently consider familiar in both their behaviours and within their culture.

For example, the original Apple iPhone, which launched in 2007, quickly gained mass market adoption because it provided an ideal blend of familiarity in terms of form and size with unique and revolutionary technical features such as a touchscreen user interface and the lack of a physical keyboard. It allowed for a bigger screen, which then opened up greater versatility for other functions such as videos and gaming etc.

Technical advancements such as the inclusion of an accelerometer saw the advent of screen switching between portrait and landscape formats, a novel feature which is now ubiquitous among smartphones.

Drawing It All Together

In the pursuit of creating commercially successful products, it's important to consider and implement the factors of 'familiarity' and 'uniqueness' in the design. An all too familiar product, with no differentiation from its competitors, will be less able to attract consumers in their final purchasing decision. And a product which is unique but not familiar enough to consumers in terms of its style and functionality may be discounted even before they reach their final purchasing decision. Critically, the 'unique' elements of the product need to deliver a surprising spark of emotion to the consumer which drives their curiosity and desire to own and use it. Over time, if the product continues to deliver above the expectations of its claimed performance, it'll build brand loyalty with the consumer, who may then consider future repeat purchases. They may also help to drive brand awareness by becoming an advocate for the product, sharing reviews and recommending it to family, friends and colleagues.

44 RESPECT THE TRENDS

'Trends, like horses, are easier to ride in the direction they are already going.'

JOHN NAISBITT

What Is the Rule?

The products you create need to be aesthetically relevant and engaging when they launch to market. Consumer tastes and aesthetic preferences follow the current trends in that particular industry and region of the world. These trends are in constant flux, so by making the effort to monitor their evolution, you place yourself in a strong position from which to adapt and adjust the form, colours and graphics of your products for greater appeal and commercial success.

The Problem

Trends can influence the many ingredients which go into the manufacturing process and result in a product for sale, but they are often driven by aesthetics, whether it's combinations of shapes and colours, surface finishes or materials. Like it or not, your product has a style or aesthetic which is often driven by function. But the visual element of a product is what creates an emotional response in consumers. As human beings, we use all of our senses, but we are predominantly driven by sight; we see colours and shapes before we even read text. This is why aesthetics are so powerful.

Trends reflect our tendency to flock together. They will often grow as more and more people start to follow them, as we feel more comfortable when we assimilate with the masses. So, here's the problem from a design perspective. If your product doesn't reflect the trend of the day, then you simply won't sell and be successful if mass market adoption is your aim.

But what provokes a trend? We start with the drivers, or macroeconomic factors – whether they are political, technological, social or economic. Drivers influence and change our beliefs. If beliefs change, then behaviours follow. If the amount of shared behaviour reaches critical mass, it becomes a trend. If the trend continues to grow and permeate across different sections of society and industries, it can become a 'global trend', which itself can become a driving macroeconomic factor. These factors can be visualised as connections in a virtuous circle, as shown in Figure 44.1 below. I have always found this framework useful when monitoring and analysing the external environment because it helps to connect the dots.

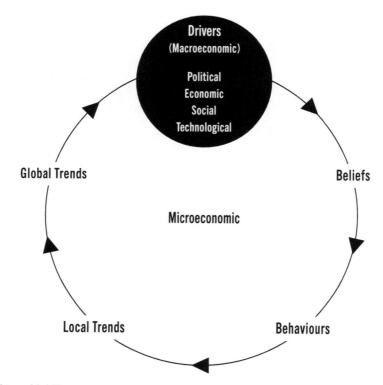

Figure 44.1 The circle of influence between macroeconomic and microeconomic factors

The Solution

Throw yourself into research. Explore trends occurring in different markets. Visit galleries and artists, as artists are often at the start of cultural changes which influence trends. Use trend research sources or agencies if you have the budget for subscriptions. Visit retail stores, but beware that these will be influenced by the trends rather than driving them, so they may not be as 'hot' when your product launches in the future. You can also use observation and your connections to pick up on trends, for example, if you see or hear of common behaviours from a few different sources. Note that trends are often cyclical. Some trends never disappear; they simply lower and then rise every few years.

Map out and monitor these trends using a digital tool or wall space in your design studio. Build this research as an ongoing live project to monitor the growth and progression of the trends which are specifically relevant to your business and products. The tool can be referenced at the beginning of any new project and at key stages of development. Over time, the tool will become more valuable as more insights from different sources are accumulated. And where insights are common or repeated, clusters of bubbles will form where different sources of information converge, suggesting a set of beliefs, behaviours or trends are emerging. This all gives extra weight and confidence to your analysis and future predictions.

A great benefit of trends is that they can help inspire the design creation process and result in an even greater array of ideas for your products. Trends can set you and your product apart from others, increasing market leverage and sales. It's no coincidence that most fashion and lifestyle brands update their product colours and graphics at least every six months. They are following the trends and fighting to remain relevant to their shoppers and consumers. However, it's also important to recognise that depending on your product type and the industry you work within, it may not be possible to capitalise on the current marketplace trends if it takes you longer than six months to launch. It's also worth considering whether you want your product to align with current trends. If your company is the market leader, then you're in a position to create the trends as other companies follow your movements.

Drawing It All Together

It's clear that styling and aesthetics offer pleasure to the consumer and improve their experience. Function is not enough. We can see that their choices are shaped by the pull of trends when we look at the fashion industry. It's important to listen to this inbuilt human desire and do our research to make sure new products reflect what's currently appealing. But trends change, so it's also critical to monitor their evolution in order to shape your new designs. You don't want to lose favour by taking your eye off the ball.

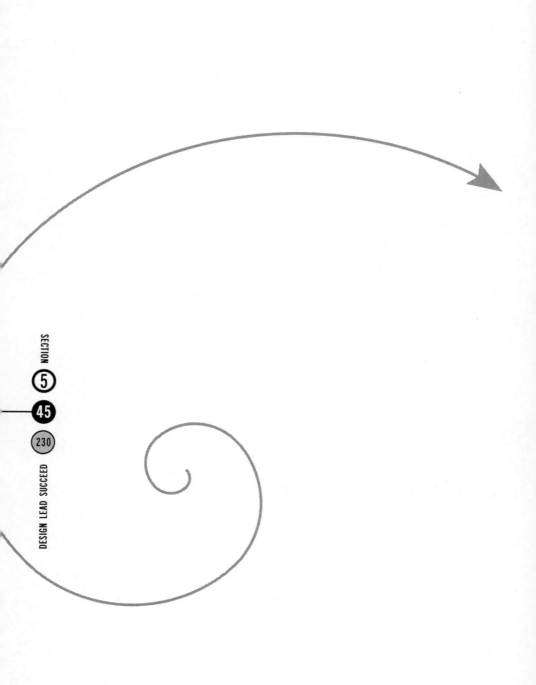

45 EXPLORE IDEAS USING SEQUENTIAL SKETCHING

'You only design by going against received ideas.'
KARL LAGERFELD

What Is the Rule?

As designers, we often need to test and explore ideas to see if they're worth pursuing. Sequential sketching is a very simple but highly effective method for exploring a design concept. By evolving each iteration of the idea on the sketch pad, you can quickly work out what works and what doesn't. Instil this approach among your team for greater creativity and quality of execution.

The Problem

Ideas can occur to us at any time. Sometimes we have moments of inspiration, but as designers, the ideas often begin to come to us as soon as we apply ourselves to a problem. However, unless you are a genius, the ideas will probably not arrive in your mind as fully finished and functioning solutions. They will require interrogating to see whether they stand up as robust products in the real world. So, in order to resolve the idea through to a finished concept design, you need a method of quickly exploring it.

The Solution

So, you have an idea. You need to quickly explore all of its possibilities and follow it through to a reasonable conclusion. This is when sequential sketching comes into play. But how and why does it work? Your mind races at pace, and ideas can keep flowing when you are 'in the zone'. Ideally, if you are fairly proficient at sketching on paper, then you will be able to keep up with your mind as you translate intangible ideas into tangible representations on paper. There are infinite possible variants to every conceived idea, but by using the approach of sequential sketches, slight variants around each idea on a connected path, it will be easier for your thoughts to continue flowing. You'll evolve your design using small changes rather than moving off on jagged tangents by asking big questions and making leaps. It also means that your process of design – the evolution of your thoughts on the product – is visible, as the sketches form a storyboard: a clearly connected sequence of events. This is a great reference point for you when looking back at how you got to the end product, when starting the process again or when showing your design to colleagues. It was not until I'd graduated and was working as a young designer that a design director kindly explained this approach and its benefits to me.

It's helpful to use the sketch of your initial idea (or of an existing product) as a standard reference point – or underlay – on which to build all other sequential sketches. This helps to speed up the process as it ensures consistency of design proportions and visual perspective. This is important as it allows easy comparison between colleagues' ideas and it avoids us becoming distracted by differences in style and size, which might influence our decisions unfairly.

Let me walk you through the process. Take the underlay, sketch over it and start your ideation. Then create a second sketch using the same underlay, but this time, change only one thing about your design. The change could be the shape, the angle, a feature or the fixtures. Then repeat, and repeat and repeat. Let your mind flow with ideas upon ideas. Imagine all the different variables and solutions to the problem which you are trying to resolve. But try to only change one variable at a time. This way, after a period of time, when you stand back and review your sketch journey – whether you are alone or, ideally, with colleagues – you will notice what change works best. It is harder to distinguish this if you are changing too many parts of the design each time.

One benefit of this technique is that it allows others to see opportunities in your sketches and ideation journey. It is like opening up the workings of your mind to observers to get a second opinion. This often results in stronger solutions and even more variants to explore.

However, sequential sketching does have some limits. Some ideas and lines of investigation cannot be fully resolved, or they finish at dead ends following the sequential sketching method. Sometimes it is then necessary to explore the ideas in 3D with models due to their complexity. You should also consider using other ideation techniques in combination with sequential sketches. When ideas are drying up, try brainstorming tools such as SCAMPER or 6Ms, for example. This will help to form the starting point for a new initial idea.

Drawing It All Together

Sequential sketching, as a method of working, will make filtering your ideas a lot quicker and easier at review stage. This is one of the key rules that I teach to students and designers, and it has a massive impact on their output. It will also be simpler to go back to your original sketches and start from where you left off because the ideation journey is clearly evident. But can you break this rule? Of course you can! It's a creative process. Sometimes, the desire to sketch to final form will flow, so just let go and see what comes out on paper.

Also, this approach is not just restricted to sketching. It's of great benefit to design development activities throughout the full breadth of the design creation process. For example, it can be used in the refinement of pre-production prototypes through testing, the further refinement of post-production samples and in final improvements to production tooling.

46 SIMULATE YOUR CONCEPTS

'Rather than designing a virtual component and then testing it on the computer for aerodynamic efficiency, we now had the option to ask the software to tell us what the best shape was.'

CHRIS BOARDMAN

What Is the Rule?

Your product needs to provide an unparalleled experience to the consumer if it's going to have a chance of widespread adoption. For your concepts to repeatedly realise their true potential, it's hugely beneficial to test early and often in the design creation process. Computer simulation software will help you to predict the performance of both aesthetics and function. In the long-run, this will reduce your investment of money and time as well as opening up unexpected, enlightening and paradigm-shifting lines of enquiry.

The Problem

In the pursuit of building beautiful products, a successful outcome is never guaranteed. When you look behind a brilliant product, it's littered with any number of discarded design concepts, conceived and iterated on from the very beginning and throughout the journey of development. Concepts are wonderful because they are abstract vehicles for visually exploring ideas, but it's hard to pinpoint which ones are worth keeping. Realising the true potential of a concept often means turning the intangible into the tangible by creating a physical product which will allow you to test functional and aesthetic characteristics. Many concepts don't survive this journey of development. Those that do survive must evolve and often combine with other concepts, blending the strengths of both entities to create a stronger whole.

It's often very difficult to understand what the main problems are with a product when designing a new concept. But learning of their flaws and weaknesses early on can significantly reduce development time. Extensive physical testing also helps in improving quality and user experience because you're working in the three-dimensional world where the laws of physics apply rather than the two-dimensional medium of a drawn concept. If concepts aren't explored and tested enough, or even at all with the assumption that they'll perform well in the hands of the consumer, then major problems such as component fatigue and failure may occur when launched in the market. To arrive at the best solution, you'll need to be confident that the product withstands extensive usage and is reliable. By using multiple test phases, which will provide opportunities to iterate, you'll uncover unforeseen opportunities to alter and improve a concept before production commences. However, note that there are often limitations to how many physical tests can be completed due to time constraints and budget.

The Solution

When physical testing becomes too time-consuming or prohibitive for reasons such as safety or budget, the option of computer simulation tests should be considered. Simulations model the three-dimensional world with programmed algorithms to predict the laws of physics. This allows discrete events, where your product would be used, to be simulated accurately. For example, in a previous role I utilised simulations that modelled how passengers moved around a train carriage to inform its design.

Arguably, the entire design creation process could be completed through computer simulations. However, they are, by their very nature, only a representation of very controlled conditions. Real-life validation tests are therefore necessary to confirm your findings, using physical samples or prototypes, as they capture the infinite variables of the physical world. Digital simulation technology is catching up though.

Simulations help you to configure the optimum design solutions in the minimum time and with the minimum expense. It can help you gain perspective on an issue in much the same way that standing back from any situation does, providing an independent opinion on what's happening during the interaction between user and product. It can also make you more objective and thorough in your analysis.

Start by considering the needs that your product must fulfil then identify simulation options to test its ability to satisfy those needs. In this way, simulations can help to develop the concept to its true potential.

Consider the following aspects when looking to incorporate computer simulations into your design creation process:

Develop hypotheses – Plan your testing work methodically and develop hypotheses around the most influential features of your design creation. This is a good way to monitor and control the process of investigation. Through rigorous testing, you may conclude that only a few of your hypotheses were true, but that may then guide you to the next successive round of tests with further hypotheses to explore.

Don't forget physical validation – Simulate using simulation software such as finite element analysis (FEA) or computational fluid dynamics (CFD), then validate your results by testing with a physical model where this is feasible. This process helps to confirm the real-world accuracy and validity of your simulation work.

Calibrate your results – Wherever possible, it is important to try and improve the accuracy of the simulated test results by calibrating them with the material properties and values of the physical world tests.

Utilise AI software – Use AI software during the process to simulate alternate lines of exploration. In this way, some simulation software packages dramatically reduce testing time by way of 'machine learning'. They calculate all conceivable options and whittle the options down to the optimum solutions. I've used this methodology on past projects with great results. It's commonly used in the motorsport industry for Formula One car aerodynamics.

Gain manufacturing insights – Simulation software also helps to predict and refine the manufacturing process and equipment before investment has been signed off. For example, it can identify the probable behaviour of polymers during the injection moulding process, which can inform improvements in the product design in terms of durability and material waste reduction.

Employ simulation specialists – If you have the money, you could task an external company or institution with investigating your hypotheses using simulations. It could also be set up as a student project within a design institution if you have a smaller budget.

Assess the appearance of your product – Arguably, visual rendering, virtual reality and augmented reality software create simulations of final appearance and finish. Using this, you can simulate and test for functional aspects and aesthetics (the two cannot be separated). However, aesthetics can be removed and controlled by removing elements such as colour between different tests of physical prototypes.

Drawing It All Together

Becoming more 'objective' rather than 'subjective' in your assessment of design challenges can help you to weed out the gremlins in your concepts and arrive more quickly at a great solution. An excellent method for increased objectivity is the use of simulation software which will test your concept, allowing it to reach its full potential. These software packages can simulate almost any real-world scenario, predicting a likely outcome. But beware: the results are only as accurate as the numbers you put into the simulation. So, take care to calibrate your simulation model to real life. The best solution is always a combination of simulation and physical tests to validate your findings. Moreover, just because nothing shows up in your testing, doesn't necessarily mean that there are no issues to resolve. It can also mean that you haven't created the correct testing conditions from which to identify them.

47 FIND THE BEST FACTORY FOR YOUR NEEDS

'Modern design should master the machine
for the service of man.'

EDGAR KAUFMANN, JR.

What Is the Rule?

To design the best product is not enough! For it to be a success, it needs to be created – brought to life – in the most effective way. Seek to partner with the best manufacturers which meet the needs and budget of your current business situation.

The Problem

Formula One is the pinnacle of motorsport. It brings man and machine together in unison. And, more often than not, it is the best performing car which dictates which driver wins. The design is important in this respect, of course, but the value delivered by the build quality and capabilities of the manufacturing team cannot be underestimated. I believe the same theory applies to the design of your product. The best factories will build the best products.

But how can 'best' be defined? Can a factory be the best across the full breadth of manufacturing requirements? Possibly. 'Best' certainly comes with associated financial costs, however, which may or may not make the factory an option for you depending on the current situation of your business. Importantly, the factory needs to be the best fit for your business situation and future product.

The Solution

There are many organisations that operate a vertical business model which involves ownership of their manufacturing facilities, providing them with greater flexibility and control of costs. This option is becoming more attractive for some businesses when they consider that the cost savings from shifting production to other countries with lower labour costs are now diminishing. Manufacturing closer to market also allows for quicker order replenishment and cheaper transport of materials and products with the associated reduction in CO_2 emissions. Having previously worked for such an organisation, I know there are advantages to this approach in the right circumstances. The production line where I worked was only a short walk from my design studio. This enabled convenient access for discussions and resolution of manufacturing issues between design, engineering and production teams. This is in contrast to companies who have their manufacturing overseas. This leads to much more complex communications between parties across different businesses and regions of the world. When kept in-house, manufacturing methods can also be held exclusively and protected from copying, meaning a sustained advantage can be held over competitors. The main drawback of in-house manufacturing is that a business takes on the additional overhead costs and all of the associated risks and liabilities of the production process, such as labour, equipment, maintenance etc.

If your organisation does not have the facilities to manufacture your product, you will be partnering with external factories. Here are some of the key considerations when selecting and working with a factory to ensure the best quality of output:

Are they ethical and compliant? – It needs to be excellent in the non-negotiable aspects of corporate responsibility with policies around anti-slavery, no child labour and compliance with all other regulations that must be audited. You are in it together with the factory and your reputation is on the line.

What are their design quality and manufacturing capabilities? – Consider the areas which hold the key to the successful execution of your design. How does the factory operate? The manufacturing processes they use can make or break the design. What are their quality control processes? Do they have a quality plan in place? If the build quality is not great, the product will not perform well in market. Quality issues could lead to returns and financial losses.

Do you have a suitable contract? – Any working relationship with a factory needs to be grounded in an agreed contract. It's critical to get the contract in place at the very start of the project, before any work begins, to clear up roles and responsibilities. This will help to maintain a strong working partnership. Insist on ownership of all IP arising from the development of your design creation and the collaboration, and this should be confirmed in the contract. However, this is not always possible if you are relying on a lot of the design and engineering capabilities of the factory for the creation of the product.

How will you collaborate and what is the culture like? – How does the factory collaborate and work with inventors and designers? Can you find examples of other organisations that they have worked with for recommendations? You will find it difficult to discover everything about a potential factory until you actually work with them, but it is good to hear about someone's previous experiences. This might uncover details such as how they handle costing, whether they follow lead times and if they honour project plans. Depending on the size of your product range, you could begin the working relationship with a small production run of a single product to assess the situation before you make any further commitments. And what about the culture of their organisation? This is heavily influenced by the owner and leadership team. Ideally, they will have an open-minded approach to any project with a passionate engineering team. This will influence how far they are willing to work to push technological boundaries for the benefit of the product. Will they acquire and invest in new capabilities and new materials when necessary, something that will also raise the standard of their operation? The best factories have better facilities, engineers and technicians. They will be better at solving all of the technical issues you will face during development. This means the final product will better resemble what you imagined it would be.

Drawing It All Together

By finding the best factory for your project, you'll benefit by providing your product the best possible chance of commercial success once it's launched. Maintaining a great relationship with the factory is vital, and you should put continuous effort into building trust, respect and rapport for long-term success.

48 JOURNAL EACH PROJECT'S JOURNEY

'Consumers pretend that they're rational and careful and thoughtful about the stuff they buy. Actually they're not. Instead they rely on stories. Stories matter.'

SETH GODIN

What Is the Rule?

Charting the story of your product's creation as it unfolds, in a design journal, serves as an invaluable tool. It will help you to sell the benefits of the product and project to the various internal and external stakeholders throughout the creative process while saving time in your communication method and capturing valuable imagery for marketing purposes.

The Problem

Throughout the creative journey of a design project, your team could be called on to provide project updates at any moment. You might need to justify the purpose and value of the project or explain requests for additional funding to various stakeholders who want their return on investment. These are essential crux points for your project, so they must be taken seriously, but they also take time, effort and resources away from your team. There needs to be a quick and easy way of fulfilling these requests to ensure the future success of your project.

The Solution

Immense value lies in creating and maintaining a live document as a type of journal for recording each design project. This should chart the journey of the project, with details and rationale for each design decision throughout the creative process. Often, words are not enough to convey the product updates, so you should aim for a design journal document that's filled with imagery. These might include concept ideation sketches, design research finding charts, CAD renderings, testing photographs etc. This will provide you with an excellent and complete presentation when you need to update the executive team and senior leadership.

Consider the following aspects when creating and using the design journal document:

Assign responsibility immediately – It's important to assign responsibility for updating the document to the lead design manager or designer on the project so that it doesn't fall between the cracks and get forgotten. Get the document rolling as soon as the project starts so that no detail of its journey is missed.

Use a template – For efficiency, it makes sense to create a template version of this document for ease of future replication.

Take lots of photographs – Remember to take photographs at each stage of the creative journey to document its evolution. These will serve as invaluable marketing assets on social media when the product launches to market.

Use it to save time in meetings – Format information and images in the document so that they can easily be dropped into documents and communications used in other meetings and presentations. This will save the design team precious time in sharing assets.

Use it to brief other teams – It will also provide you with a great tool for handover when different teams need to be brought up to speed as and when they join the project at a later stage. For example, this might be a great way to introduce marketing to the product as they can utilise a lot of this information to develop a launch campaign.

Use it to avoid patent infringement – The document serves as an excellent tool to update and brief the legal team or patent attorneys during a design project when it is necessary to begin prior art searches. This will support your efforts to mitigate the risk of patent infringement when the product launches to market.

Use it to share learnings internally – You might be quite surprised at how often you are asked to revisit past projects and share learnings, which this document can help with. The document could also form a foundation for your research when developing new versions of the product.

Use it as a case study for external presentations – Once you've completed the project, the document could serve as a case study for external presentations – at design conferences, for example – to illustrate your and your company's work.

Drawing It All Together

Grasp the opportunity to build the story of your design projects by journaling the journey as you progress, with the benefit of freshly recorded information and captured photographs. This disciplined approach to recording the journey 'little and often' will pay dividends in the end as it avoids the necessity to create additional retrospective documents for the purposes of internal and external stakeholder communications. The document will also serve as a visual story of the value that your design team creates and a starting point of reference for any new product journey. Importantly, the document also aids the wider business, and the marketing team in particular, in communicating the design creation story of the product to the consumer, helping to increase engagement and brand awareness.

CONCLUSION

This book aims to help develop the design leadership skills of anyone who's currently a designer and considering embarking on their leadership journey, as well as the experienced leader looking to add a few skills to their repertoire.

I hope you've benefitted and continue to benefit from using this book as a reference guide as and when you need support. The five sections of this book, which aim to build your knowledge sequentially – from 'How to Know Yourself, Your Organisation and Your Industry' in Section 1 through to 'How to Elevate the Design Creation Process' in Section 5 – will help to propel you and your team towards maximum creativity. Creativity is a difficult entity to objectively measure. Ruth Noller developed a pretty good theory based on research when she suggested that the level of creativity generated could be measured as a function of knowledge (cognition and memory), imagination (divergent production) and evaluation (convergent production and evaluation). And all these factors are multiplied by the level of creative attitude:

Creativity = Creative Attitude (Knowledge, Imagination, Evaluation)

If we consider this formula, we can see the direct influence which design leadership can have on the level of creativity in any given situation. For example, by setting up a creative culture within a design team and organisation, the creative attitude is improved. In fact, all 48 rules within this book directly influence either one or a combination of the factors in this formula.

This book contains 48 rules, but it doesn't mean that we should stop there. Considering the speed at which tools powered by artificial intelligence have become available to designers to help aid the creative process, I'm confident that new rules will need to evolve and be defined in order to better lead the design process. This constant striving to improve and iterate on our current approaches can only benefit our discipline. Ultimately, it'll result in better leaders, better products and happier design teams. But also, remember that everyone is unique in terms of their own style and approach to design and leadership. You must find your own way, treading your own path and creating your own unique rules. Take the 48 rules in this book and adapt them to suit your specific needs. Rules are also there to be broken.

ACKNOWLEDGEMENTS

Writing this book has had to be a solitary experience for substantial chunks of time, but I'm very proud to say that the completed book has been realised due to a wider team effort of individuals who have supported me and that I must now thank.

I feel blessed to have found Sarah Busby, my development and copy editor, on my writing journey. Her mentorship, patience and encouragement throughout the book's development have been invaluable. As a designer, drawing has always come more naturally to me than writing, so I thank Sarah for all her great suggested improvements to the book and for everything she has taught me along the way.

A huge thank you to Clare Baggaley who has been wonderful to collaborate with in her creation of the cover and typesetting of the book. And thanks to Krista Nelson for carrying out a comprehensive proofread.

Thank you to my good friend Garry McKenna for being a critical and honest sounding board, mentor, and generous provider of inspiring ideas, especially on the home straight when I was pulling the book together, reminding me to consider the branding aspects of the book in our biweekly coffee shop catch-ups.

Thank you to my friend Duncan Shaw for coaching me exactly when I needed it with his acute sensitivity to aspects of a project's strategic vision! He helped me unblock my thought process in the early stages as I wrestled with what the next best step should be in the writing process.

I'm forever thankful for having been blessed with such devoted and supportive parents, Joan and Burney. My Dad has been the catalyst for this book throughout the whole process. When anything was more enticing to me than putting pen to paper, my dad would continue to pepper me with ideas and suggestions which kept the fire lit beneath me and maintained my momentum.

During my career in the design industry, I've been very fortunate to work with many wonderful and influential people. So, I must thank all of my previous employers and colleagues who have helped to shape my approach to design.

And finally, a special thanks to Starbucks for all the caffe lattes that pulled me through the countless mornings of my writing routine. Without these, the book might still be a work in progress!

FURTHER READING

Here are some open access databases that I would recommend exploring in relation to Chapter 37, *Harness the Power of Literature Reviews.*

- PubMed Central (ncbi.nlm.nih.gov/pmc/)
- Semantic Scholar (semanticscholar.org)
- Google Scholar (scholar.google.com)
- CORE (core.ac.uk)
- Social Science Research Network (ssrn.com)

REFERENCES

Rule 1 – Discover Who You Are
Krishnamurti, J. *The First and Last Freedom*. Ebury Publishing, 2013.

'*Take the MBTI Instrument*'. The Myers & Briggs Foundation. 2023. https://www.myersbriggs.org/my-mbti-personality-type/take-the-mbti-instrument

Rule 2 – Find the Secret Sauce
Dore, F., Kouyoumjian, G., Sarrazin, H., & Sheppard, B. '*McKinsey Quarterly – The Business Value of Design*'. McKinsey & Company. October 25, 2018. https://www.mckinsey.com/capabilities/mckinsey-design/our-insights/the-business-value-of-design

Strohmeier, B.R. '*The Leadership Principles Used by Jack Welch as He Re-Energized, Revolutionized, and Reshaped General Electric*'. Journal of Leadership Studies, vol. 5, no. 2 (January 1999), p21. https://journals.sagepub.com/doi/10.1177/107179199900500203

Rule 3 – Understand What Worked Before
Churchill, W.S. *Churchill by Himself: In His Own Words*. Rosetta Books, 2013.

Rule 4 – Track Your Environment
Porter, M.E. *Competitive Strategy: Techniques for Analysing Industries and Competitors*. Macmillan Publishing, 1980.

Walsh, B. *The Score Takes Care of Itself: My Philosophy of Leadership*. Penguin Books, 2009.

Rule 5 – Put People First
Holtz, L. *Winning Every Day: The Game Plan For Success*. Collins Business, 1998.

Robbins, T. '*Discover the 6 Human Needs – These Core Needs Drive Every Decision You* Make'. www.tonyrobbins.com. 2023. https://www.tonyrobbins.com/mind-meaning/do-you-need-to-feel-significant

Rule 6 – Nurture a Positive and Creative Culture
The famous quote, "Culture eats strategy for breakfast!" is commonly attributed to the management guru Peter Drucker, but there is no written evidence that he actually said it. However, it does encapsulate his thinking about the primacy of culture and it became a commonly used phrase in business thinking to convey this idea.

Knight, P. *Shoe Dog: A Memoir by the Creator of Nike*. Simon & Schuster, 2016.

Nike mission statement. 2023. https://about.nike.com/en

Patagonia purpose statement. 2023. https://eu.patagonia.com/gb/en/ownership

DESIGN LEAD SUCCEED

Rule 7 – Make the Mission Clear and Get the Team Onboard

Adidas purpose statement. 2023. https://www.adidas-group.com/en/about/profile

Kounkel, S., Main, A., O'Brien, D., & Stephan, A.R. *'Purpose Is Everything: How Brands That Authentically Lead with Purpose Are Changing the Nature Of Business Today'* Deloitte Insights, 15 October 2019. https://www2.deloitte.com/us/en/insights/topics/marketing-and-sales-operations/global-marketing-trends/2020/purpose-driven-companies.html

Senge, P.M. *The Fifth Discipline: The Art and Practice of the Learning Organization.* Cornerstone, 1990.

Rule 8 – Set Shared Principles

De Jong, C.W., ed. *Ten Principles for Good Design: Dieter Rams.* Prestel, 2017.

Goens, G.A. *Civility Lost: The Media, Politics, and Education.* Rowman & Littlefield Publishers, 2019.

Buffet, W. *'Intelligence, Energy, Integrity'.* 2023. https://www.youtube.com/shorts/0iLY9gzvFwA

Rule 9 – Eliminate Egos

De Bono, E. *How to Have a Beautiful Mind.* Vermilion, 2004.

Freud, S. *The Ego and the Id.* Hogarth Press, 1927.

Rule 10 – Build Trust

Ziglar, Z. *Zig Ziglar's Treasury of Life Lessons.* Sound Wisdom, 2022.

Rule 11 – Assemble Your A Team

Collins, J. *Good to Great: Why Some Companies Make the Leap... and Others Don't.* Collins Business, 2001.

Rule 12 – Know Your Team's Personalities

Johansson, F. *The Medici Effect: Breakthrough Insights at the Intersection of Ideas, Concepts, and Cultures.* Harvard Business Press, 2006.

Understand Myself Personality Assessment. 2023. https://www.understandmyself.com

Rule 13 – Set Out Your Team Structure

Gerber, M.E. *The E Myth Revisited: Why Most Small Businesses Don't Work and What to Do About It.* HarperCollins, 1995.

Peters, S. *The Chimp Paradox: The Mind Management Programme for Confidence, Success and Happiness.* Vermilion, 2011.

Rule 14 – Define Roles and Responsibilities
Lavin, J. *Management Secrets of the New England Patriots: From 'Patsies' to Two-Time Super Bowl Champs, Vol 1.* Pointer Press, 2005.

Rule 15 – Help Your Team to Reach Their Maximum Potential
Holtz, L. *Winning Every Day: The Game Plan for Success.* HarperCollins, 1998.

Rule 16 – Establish a Culture of Learning
Frederick, C. *'Continuous Learning'.* Motor-Age, vol. 135 (April 2016), pp. 15–16.

Little, J., ed. *Bruce Lee Jeet Kune Do: Bruce Lee's Commentaries on The Martial Way.* Tuttle Publishing, 1997.

Tee Ng, P. *'The Learning Organisation and the Innovative Organisation'.* Human Systems Management, vol. 23, no. 2 (January 2004), pp. 93–100.

Rule 17 – Advise Team Members Sensitively
Bell, C.R. *Managers as Mentors: Building Partnerships for Learning.* Berrett-Koehler Publishers, 2002.

Centre for Creative Leadership. *'Use Situation-Behaviour-Impact (SBI)™ to Understand Intent'.* Centre for Creative Leadership. 2023. https://www.ccl.org/articles/leading-effectively-articles/closing-the-gap-between-intent-vs-impact-sbii

Rule 18 – Find Balance and Protect Your Resilience
Impelman, C. *'The Second Most Important Thing Is Balance'.* Coach John Wooden Pyramid of Succcess. March 13, 2019. https://www.thewoodeneffect.com/the-second-most-important-thing-is-balance

Rule 19 – Widen Your Network and Develop Allies
Mortenson, G., & Relin, D.O. *Three Cups of Tea.* Penguin Books, 2008.

Rule 20 – Delegate and Empower
Jenks, J.M., & Kelly, J.M. *Don't Do. Delegate! : The Secret Power of Successful Managers.* Kogan Page, 1987.

Rule 21 – More Directing, Less Designing
Lowe, J. *Jack Welch Speaks: Wit and Wisdom from the World's Greatest Business Leader.* Wiley, 2008.

Rule 22 – Manage Your and Your Team's Time

Lakein, A. *How to Get Control of Your Time and Your Life*. Gower, 1984.

Rule 23 – Direct Through Design Briefs

Wood, J. *Dictionary of Quotations*. Frederick Warne & Co, 1893.

Rule 24 – Guide Your Team with the Marketing Claims

Wheeler, A. *Designing Brand Identity: An Essential Guide for the Whole Branding Team*. Wiley, 2017.

'Marketing without design is lifeless. Design without marketing is mute.' Used with permission from the author Von Glitschka.

Rule 25 – Shepherd Ideas Towards Solutions

Knoll Studio. *'Warren Platner'*. Platner Collection. 2023. https://www.knoll.com/story/shop/original-design-platner-collection

Rule 26 – Utilise Design Reviews for Quality Control

De Jong, C.W., ed. *Ten Principles for Good Design: Dieter Rams*. Prestel, 2017.

ISO Standards. *'Benefits of Standards'*. ISO Standards. 2023. https://www.iso.org/benefits-of-standards.html

Rule 27 – Look Back, Learn and Then Leap Forward

de Bono, E. *'Six Thinking Hats'*. The de Bono Group. 2023. https://www.debonogroup.com/services/core-programs/six-thinking-hats

The famous quote, 'We do not learn from experience, we learn from reflecting on experience' is commonly attributed to the philosopher John Dewey, but there is no written evidence that he actually said it. However, it does encapsulate his thinking from his book 'Art as Experience'.
Dewey, J. *Art as Experience*. Perigee, 1980.

Rule 28 – Search for Simplicity

Jensen, B. *'Make it Simple! How Simplicity Could Become Your Ultimate Strategy'*. Strategy & Leadership, vol. 25, no. 2 (February 1997), pp.35–39.

Lesté-Lasserre, C. *'Lizards That Lost Their Legs Re-Evolved Them as the Climate Got Wetter'*. New Scientist. 11 November 2020. https://www.newscientist.com/article/2259415-lizards-that-lost-their-legs-re-evolved-them-as-the-climate-got-wetter

Little, J., ed. *Bruce Lee Jeet Kune Do: Bruce Lee's Commentaries on The Martial Way*. Tuttle Publishing, 1997.

Rule 29 – Establish Operational Excellence
Christensen, C.M. *The Innovator's Dilemma: When New Technologies Cause Great Firms to Fail.* Harvard Business Review Press, 1997.

Pulos, A.J. *The American Design Adventure.* MIT Press, 1988.

Rule 30 – Take Charge of Your Financial Planning
Rumsfeld, D. *Public Statements of Donald H. Rumsfeld, Secretary of Defense, 2001.* Historical Office, Office of the Secretary of Defense, 2001.

Rule 31 – Protect Your Team in Relation to Intellectual Property
Bergmann, I., Butzke, D., Walter, L., Fuerste, J.P., Moehrle, M.G., & Erdmann, V.A. *'Evaluating the Risk of Patent Infringement by Means of Semantic Patent Analysis: The Case of DNA Chips'.* R&D Management, vol. 38, no. 5 (October 2008), pp. 550–562.

Gatto, J.G., Blaise, B.C. and Esplin, D.B. *'Worlds.com Saber-Rattling Portends a Trend in Virtual World and Video Game Patents'.* Intellectual Property & Technology Law Journal, vol. 21, no. 5 (May 2009), pp. 8–12.

Gilson, D.G. *'Online Searching of Patents Databases: a Southern African Perspective'.* The Electronic Library, vol. 9, no. 4/5 (April 1991), pp. 257–262.

Higgins, B.W. *'Adding Business Value: A Strategy for Identifying and Patenting Environment-Related Inventions and Avoiding Patent Infringement'.* Business Strategy and the Environment, vol. 12, no. 2 (2003), pp. 118–128.

Hubbard, M. & Brooks, J. *'The Effect of Seagate on Patent Infringement Risk Management Strategies'.* Intellectual Property & Technology Law Journal, vol. 22, no. 3 (March 2010).

Lang, J.C. *'Management of Intellectual Property Rights – Strategic Patenting'.* Journal of Intellectual Capital, vol. 2, no. 1 (March 2001), pp. 8–26.

Lunn, J. *'An Empirical Analysis of Firm Process and Product Patenting'.* Applied Economics, vol. 19, no. 6 (June 1987), pp. 743–751.

Messner, R. *All 14 Eight-Thousanders.* The Crowood Press, 1988.

Mukherjee, A. & Ray, A. *'Unsuccessful Patent Application and Cooperative R&D'.* Journal of Economics, vol. 97, no. 3 (April 2009), pp. 251–263.

World Intellectual Property Organization. *'IP Litigation Costs'.* WIPO Magazine. February 2010. https://www.wipo.int/export/sites/www/wipo_magazine/en/pdf/2010/wipo_pub_121_2010_01.pdf

DESIGN LEAD SUCCEED

Rule 32 – Control the Creative Direction

Adidas. *'Q&A Adidas X Parley Partnership'*. Adidas Group. 2023. https://www.adidas-group.com/media/filer_public/16/29/16299d3c-ad48-4f62-a8ef-c44c25fa4e5a/adidas_x_parley_qa_website_en.pdf

Adidas. *'Adidas X Parley For The Oceans'*. Adidas Group. 2023. https://www.adidas.co.uk/parley

Adidas. *'How We Turn Plastic Bottles into Shoes: Our Partnership with Parley for the Oceans'*. Adidas Group. 2021. https://www.adidas.co.uk/blog/639412-how-we-turn-plastic-bottles-into-shoes-our-partnership-with-parley-for-the-oceans

Mamo, L. *'Design and Story'*. A Bird with a French Fry. 2016. https://abirdwithafrenchfry.com/design-and-story

Rule 33 – Always Have a Back-Up Plan

Drucker, P.F. *Managing the Non-Profit Organisation: Practices and Principles.* Butterworth-Heinemann, 1990.

Grylls, B. *Mud, Sweat, and Tears: The Autobiography.* Channel 4, 2011.

Ishikawa, K. *Guide to Quality Control.* Asian Productivity Organization, 1974.

Rule 34 – Create a Compelling and Consistent Design Language

Gilroy, D. *Little Book of Christian Louboutin.* Welbeck Publishing Group, 2021.

Van der Rohe, L.M., & Puente, M. *Conversations with Mies van der Rohe.* Princeton Architectural Press, 2008.

Rule 35 – Understand What the Consumer Values Most

Ogilvy, D. *Ogilvy on Advertising.* Prion, 2011.

Rule 36 – Consult with the Consumer During Design

Eames, C., & Eames, R. *An Eames Anthology: Articles, Film Scripts, Interviews, Letters, Notes, Speeches.* Yale University Press, 2015.

Rule 37 – Harness the Power of Literature Reviews

Newton, I. *Delphi Collected Works of Sir Isaac Newton.* Delphi Classics, 2016.

Rule 38 – Put Materials Front and Centre

Hughes, D. *'Museum Collection: The Short Life of Dupont's Corfam'.* Hagley Museum. 2023. https://www.hagley.org/librarynews/museum-collectionthe-short-life-dupont%E2%80%99s-corfam

Stach, E. *Mies van der Rohe: Space, Material and Detail.* Birkhauser, 2018.

Rule 39 – Wear Your Own Products!

Zachary, G.P. *Showstopper! The Breakneck Race to Create Windows NT and the Next Generation at Microsoft*. New York Free Press, 1994.

Rule 40 – Engage with Technical Experts

Hill, N. *Think and Grow Rich*. Vermilion, 2004.

Rule 41 – Don't Lose the Art of Sketching

James, P. *Henry Moore on Sculpture*. Macdonald, 1966.

Rule 42 – Make Hero Features Visible on Products

Chatterjee, S. '*Simple Rules for Designing BusinessModels*'. University of California Management Review, vol. 55, no. 2 (2013), pp. 97-124.

Napias, J. & Gulbenkian, S. *The World According to Karl: The Wit and Wisdom of Karl Lagerfeld*. Thames & Hudson, 2013.

Offspring. '*A History of the Air Max*'. 2022. https://www.offspring.co.uk/theplatform/sneakers/a-history-of-the-air-max

Rule 43 – Be Familiar and Unique

Hilfiger, T., & Knobler, P. *American Dreamer: My Life in Fashion & Business*. Random House Publishing Group, 2016.

Kahneman, D. *Thinking, Fast and Slow*. Penguin Books, 2012.

Rogers, E.M. *Diffusion of Innovations*. Simon & Schuster, 1962.

Sharp, B. *How Brands Grow: What Marketers Don't Know*. Oxford University Press, 2010.

Rule 44 – Respect the Trends

Naisbitt, J. *Megatrends: Ten New Directions Transforming Our Lives*. Warner Books, 1982.

Rule 45 – Explore Ideas Using Sequential Sketching

Napias, J. & Gulbenkian, S. *The World According to Karl: The Wit and Wisdom of Karl Lagerfeld*. Thames & Hudson, 2013.

Rule 46 – Simulate Your Concepts

Boardman, C. *Triumphs and Turbulence: My Autobiography*. Ebury Publishing, 2016.

Peter, M. *Computational Fluid Dynamics for Sport Simulations*. Springer, 2009.

Rule 47 – Find the Best Factory for Your Needs
Kaufmann Jr, E. *What is Modern Design?* The Museum of Modern Art, New York, 1950.

Rule 48 – Journal Each Project's Journey
Godin, S. *All Marketers Are Liars: The Power of Telling Authentic Stories in a Low-Trust World*. Portfolio, 2005.

Conclusion
Parnes, S.J., & Noller, R.B. *'Applied Creativity: The Creative Studies Project'*. The Journal of Creative Behaviour, vol. 6, no. 4 (December 1972) Part 2, p. 173.

DESIGN LEAD SUCCEED

I hope you've enjoyed reading this book. Your opinion is of great value to me, and I would be extremely grateful if you could share your feedback by providing a review of the book.

Thank you!

Find me here
www.chrisjohnson.design

Printed by Amazon Italia Logistica S.r.l.
Torrazza Piemonte (TO), Italy

54278222R00147